Words of praise for
Kissed the Girls and Made Them Cry

Lisa Bevere is one of the most transparent, direct, and right-on-target women of God I know. That's why you can trust that what she shares in this book has come from a lot of prayer, a life in order, a history of knowing God on an intimate level, and a heart devoted to helping people. At a time when women are desiring to move into all God has for them, they are being lied to and stolen from by the enemy of their souls. Lisa speaks to that problem with truth and clarity and a writing style that draws the reader in and doesn't let go. I know because once I started the book I couldn't put it down. This is a book that is desperately needed today and is a must-read for every woman, no matter what age. How I wish I'd had access to this kind of information when I was a teenager.

—STORMIE OMARTIAN
Bestselling author of *The Power of a Praying Wife*

Lisa has used God's word to shed "true light" on how God intended things to be, rather than the distorted way they have become. This is a great book for my daughter and yours and anyone who wants to find freedom in God's plans for men and women.

—STEVE ARTERBURN
Bestselling author of *Every Man's Battle*, *Avoiding Mr. Wrong*,
and *Finding Mr. Right*; and Founder of Women of Faith

Lisa deals with the heart issues of a woman's sexuality with beauty, grace, and strength. God is calling all women to reclaim their sexual destiny.

I believe Lisa has touched the heart of God and returned the garments of sexual dignity to women.

Restoration is the heart of our God and the heart of this book by Lisa Bevere.

She has written gracefully and persuasively the intentions of God's heart for purity in women's sexuality.

I highly recommend this book to any daughter of God regardless of her age. I highly recommend it as an excellent resource for youth leaders, counselors, and parents who love their daughters as well.

—DOUGLAS WEISS PH.D.
Executive Director, Heart to Heart Counseling Center

In this eye-opening book, Lisa Bevere dares to answer questions about sex that women are asking, and the vast majority of leaders are dodging. Lisa's boldness and noncompromising stand make this a "must-read" for parents and youth leaders. Most importantly, this book should be read by every woman who sincerely wants God's wisdom to live pure in a perverse world.

—NANCY ALCORN
President and Founder of Mercy Ministries of America

God has given Lisa Bevere wisdom and knowledge beyond her years, and I am very excited about this book she has written. It contains spiritually sound advise that will bless young women and help relieve them of the pressure that society puts on them. The book will also be a useful guide for mothers, youth leaders, and singles pastors.

—BETTY ROBISON
Cohost, *Life Today*

My dear friend Lisa has done it again! She touches and teaches the hearts of women with this powerful new book.

—SHERI ROSE SHEPHERD
Speaker and author of *Fit for Excellence* and *Life Is Not a Dress Rehearsal*

Lisa speaks with a knowing compassion and insight to the deepest and most secret desires of a woman's heart, and then directs her to the One True Love who alone can satisfy. She unveils the deception and lies of this world's system, bringing value and dignity back to true femininity.

—KATIE LUCE
Cofounder, Teen Mania

As one who's written often about sexual purity for men, I am constantly asked, "What about us women? We are struggling with sexual sin too!" Women need to hear from women on this issue, and Lisa is just the woman to do it. God has literally transformed my life through the Beveres' books many times. Lisa has clearly taken the time to pray, fast, and seek God's heart on this topic, so I'm confident this book will transform your life as well.

—FRED STOEKER
Coauthor, *Every Man's Battle*, *Every Woman's Desire*

THE KISSED GIRLS AND MADE THEM CRY

Why we *lose* when we *give* in

LISA BEVERE

OLIVER NELSON™

THOMAS NELSON PUBLISHERS®
Nashville

A Division of Thomas Nelson, Inc.

This book is dedicated to women young and old who long to dream but have forgotten how. Kisses were never meant to make us cry . . . unless in joy. May the words on these pages reawaken and strengthen the dream in your heart. It is my prayer you will make these truths your own and chase away every shadowy memory, fear or nightmare that stands between you and joy unspeakable. Run to the arms of your prince and enter your dream.

—*Lisa Bevere*

Contents

1 *God's Bedtime Story*

The phone rang and interrupted the usual chaos residing in a home filled with four boys set free from school for the summer.

"Hello?"

"Lisa, this is Pastor Ted. I was wondering if you would be available to speak to the girls of the high-school youth group tonight about sex?"

I froze as my mind flashed back to a recent episode of a local daytime TV talk show I'd seen while folding one of many loads of laundry. If this show was accurate, things had really changed since my high-school days. According to the TV show, even junior-high students were engaged in sexual acts I hadn't even known existed back in my early teens.

"Tonight?!" I stuttered, finding myself surprisingly nervous.

"Yes," he continued. "Here's the plan. We're going to separate the guys and the girls. I'll take the guys, and you'll have the girls in the youth room."

"John is flying in tonight. Would you mind if I checked with him first?" I asked lamely, stalling for time.

> *Even junior-high students were engaged in sexual acts I hadn't even known existed back in my early teens.*

"No, sure. Give me or the youth pastor a call back when you've decided."

I hung up . . . a little shaken. What was going on here? I travel all over the country speaking in front of large groups of women of mixed ages, so why did I have trepidation about our local high-school youth

1

group girls? I needed to get ahold of myself. After all, I was a former youth pastor's wife. I'd survived those two years more or less unscathed. Then I realized it wasn't the age group that bothered me . . . it was the subject matter.

I dialed John's cell phone. He answered at some airport in transit to our home.

"Honey, Pastor Ted wants to know if I will talk to the high-school youth-group girls tonight about sex. I don't know what I want to do. . . . I mean, you're coming home tonight, and it's kind of late notice, and I'm not even sure what I'd say to them. I mean, do you know there are a lot of girls in junior high involved in oral sex?"

My last comment was thrown in for shock value, but John was apparently unmoved. "It's fine with me. I think you should do it."

"But what am I going to say to a bunch of high-school girls? I don't even have a daughter, and I have almost no time to prepare," I argued.

"You have three hours, Lisa. I think you should go for it," John countered.

Great—he wasn't going to give me any place to hide. I heard my boys arguing and starting to get rowdy in the distant upstairs.

"No, the boys will be too wild at home for me to get anything done . . . and what should I say about sex anyway?!"

"God will show you. Listen, I'm boarding the plane. Call Ted and tell him it's fine with me."

"Well, I'm not so sure . . . but I'll let you go. Call me when you land," I muttered.

Of course it was fine with John—he wasn't the one having to do it. I hate it when I want to have an "out" and he won't give me one. I looked around his office, scanning his shelves for possible reference books as I dialed back Pastor Ted, still uncertain what I'd say.

"Pastor Ted, John is fine with it." Before I realized it, I was committed.

"Fantastic! Listen, I don't want you to overprepare. Here's the format: We will have praise and worship together. Then the girls will leave with you. They will have an opportunity to fill out three-by-five cards asking any questions that they might possibly have. You will answer their questions for the first half-hour, teach them for the next half-hour, and then let them go."

"Will I get to see the questions ahead of time?" The answer was "no." I became even more uncomfortable.

"Pastor Ted, did you know I was a *really* good heathen before becoming a Christian? I mean, it isn't like I have this wonderful testimony of purity or anything. I think someone else might be better equipped for this lecture."

"Well, I don't think you should give your testimony (since it was now obvious I didn't have one). I want you to talk about purity and give them some straight answers. You'll do great."

And then he was gone. I hung up, wondering how I'd even gotten myself involved in this. I had a zillion others things I needed to do. It meant another night away from my kids, and I certainly felt anything but qualified on the topic at that point. I ran out of John's office and gathered my four sons around for the announcement and to plead my case.

"Hey, guys, I really need your cooperation here. Pastor Ted has asked Mommy to speak to the high-school youth-group girls in three hours. I really need to prepare. I'm going to go into Daddy's office. Please, please, please let me have this time. Don't bother me unless you're bleeding. Be nice to each other. Go outside and get some fresh air or go upstairs or down in the basement, but I don't want anyone on this level of the house. I don't want to hear any arguing. Understand?"

They looked back and forth at each other and then nodded their assent. They recognized the look of a desperate woman.

I swept back into John's office and started pulling down concordances and reference materials. Out of the corner of my eye, I caught my nine-year-old son, Alec, standing outside of John's glass door looking at me. I pulled open the door.

"What is it, Alec?" I asked impatiently.

"Oh, nothing. I'm just watching you," he answered nonchalantly.

"That is not an option. Remember, you are supposed to be upstairs, downstairs, or outside! Go!" I asserted.

"Okay," he shrugged as he shuffled off.

Kids! I enclosed myself again in the semisolitude and opened up *Matthew Henry's Commentary*, but I really had no idea where to start. I pulled out my *Amplified Bible* and was reviewing all those familiar Scriptures on purity and fornication and whoremongers when the phone rang again. Now I was getting edgy. I picked it up hastily.

"Hello?"

"Hey, Lisa. It's Ted. Listen, tonight is off. We just can't make it happen this soon. But we want to be able to announce it tonight and have it happen next week. Are you going to be in town next week?"

Here was my chance! Perhaps I was scheduled to be out of town. I grabbed for my Daytimer and flipped forward a week.

"I will be home next week."

"Great—we'll do it then." And he was gone again.

I felt *some* sense of relief knowing I now had a week instead of three hours to prepare (which didn't really count as such since I hadn't even taken a shower or cooked dinner yet). I breathed a sigh of relief and let my boys know life could return to its usual rhythm, I moved forward with my day feeling a lot lighter.

Over the next week, I carried the service and its content in my heart. I really sought God and searched the Scriptures and my own heart for answers to the questions I knew I would encounter. I made an educated guess that I'd at least be asked how far it was okay "to go," as if our individual sexuality was a par course or bike race of sorts. I searched the Scriptures for a clear and definitive answer, figuring the one I had given my children when they were young wouldn't fly. After all, I was the mother who told her children Magic Johnson had gotten the HIV virus by kissing too many girls and then was surprised when they were afraid to kiss relatives goodbye. I hadn't wanted to trouble them with details when they were "so young."

I sent my oldest son to a courtship seminar when he was twelve and promised to arrange a marriage for him. I even offered to take applications for his future mate when I was out on the road. I almost had him convinced at the point when I told him how much money he would save if he weren't paying for dates. He could use it to buy a really neat car. But now I had to be serious. There would be several hundred girls who probably wouldn't go for my arranged marriage theory. I prayed in earnest:

Father, I really need an answer for these girls. I want to impart Your wisdom, not my own opinion or that of anyone else. Should I tell them it is okay to hold hands as long as they go no farther? Or perhaps You think kissing is okay? I really need to know soon.

I waited but sensed no reply to my prayer, so I got up off my face and headed for the shower. Tomorrow was D-day. As I showered, my mind wandered the paths I could walk down the next night, until I heard the Holy Spirit speak to me and focus my direction a bit.

He said to me, "You are looking for rules to restrict their behavior. Rules will not keep them. The empowerment they need must be born out of relationship. Change your focus from what they *can't* do to what they *can do.* Tell them they can go as far with their boyfriends as they are comfortable doing in front of their fathers. For fathers are the protector and guardian of the virtue for daughters."

> ᴄ~ *They can go as far with their boyfriends as they are comfortable doing in front of their fathers.*

I got excited! It wasn't about rules, and I couldn't let myself be led down that path. That would reduce the discussion to a lecture about the law and leave the teenagers powerless and me frustrated. Instead, it was about having a relationship with their heavenly Father and honoring their earthly ones. It wasn't about limitations, morals, and a code of ethics chiseled in cold stone, but of living ones penned on their hearts. I jumped out of the shower, dried off, and began to type out about six pages of notes for myself.

The following night I arrived after praise and worship had already started, feeling rather conspicuous and out of place. I obviously stood out as a woman in her forties surrounded by so many teens. It wasn't even like I could slip in undetected. I imagined the teens viewed me as another "intruder mom" come to spy on their youth group. When worship was over, the white three-by-five cards were passed out across the length and width of the auditorium for the recording of the dreaded questions. I smiled at a couple of girls sitting near me and leaned over and encouraged them to write anything they wanted. I was hoping they would be nice out of fear I might recognize their handwriting later.

"Oh, I just have a question about clothes," one volunteered innocently.

I nodded confidently and smiled, thinking to myself, *Great! I can handle a question about clothing. This will be easier than I thought. I shouldn't have gotten so bent out of shape.*

When the cards were filled out, all the females departed the main sanctuary for our destination, the youth sanctuary down the hall. There the cards were collected as the girls passed through the doorway. I couldn't help noticing how loud and rambunctious the girls were as we all made our exodus. I awkwardly waited on the sidelines as the youth leaders collected the cards from some four hundred girls and watched as these girls packed into the seats. When all the seats were full, the girls spilled out onto the floor. With all the cards collected, the stack and the microphone were handed to me, and I mounted the platform to commence the question-and-answer session.

Even the bonus of an additional week had not prepared me for the kind of questions I received that night. The first was a question as to whether or not I agreed that a certain intern at the church (named on the card) was the sexiest man alive. I replied that I did not agree. I told the girls that I thought my husband was the sexiest man alive.

The next question had to do with clothes: *Is it okay to dress sexy? How much skin can you show at any one time?*

I looked at the girls present. A lot of them were in skirts so short I had been afraid of what might happen when they sat down. Others sported bare midriffs revealing pierced navels suspended above jeans or shorts that looked as if they had been intentionally pulled down as low as possible on their hips.

For clarification I asked, "Are you wondering if I think it is okay for you to dress suggestively?"

The majority nodded their heads, pleased that I understood.

"Sure, I think it is a great idea. Go right ahead and dress like a whore if you want to attract a whoremonger. It's like fishing—the bait you use will determine what you'll catch. So if you want to hook a sleazy guy, by all means dress sleazy."

They were a little stunned, so I continued: "I'm not saying it is wrong to dress attractively or even fashionably, but dressing suggestively is only appropriate behind closed doors between a husband and his wife."

> ⌒ It's like fishing—the bait you use will determine what you'll catch.

I shared how there were things I wore alone in the bedroom with my husband that would be inappropriate to wear while walking the dog or while scrambling eggs for my four sons the following morning. Often when my children help me fold laundry, a brightly colored or oddly shaped piece of lingerie will be held up for identification, I explain it is "Mommy-Daddy" clothes. Shoulders are shrugged and the item is passed to me, "Here, you fold it. I'm not sure I know how it goes."

Another question came from the girls about what body parts were okay to pierce, to which I referenced the Bible's piercing suggestions: ears and noses (Ezek. 16:12). I recommended staying away from anything that is not made of cartilage.

> ⌒ How far is too far?

There were quite a few questions about the Bible's stance on homosexuality. Did it say anything about it? Was it wrong? How could love between any two people ever be wrong, homosexual or otherwise? As an answer, I gave them references to study for themselves and explained that the right thing (love) in the wrong setting (sexually expressed between people of the same gender) was still wrong. It is an invalid way to meet a valid need, a perversion of the valid God-ordained expression of sexual love.

There were other questions about oral sex, and some too rude, crude, and disrespectful to even mention. But then came the big one. Now, don't get me wrong. I had already encountered it a number of times, but I just kept putting it off by pushing the card to the back of the pile. It was the one most frequently recorded, closely followed by one version or another of, *Is it okay to dress sexy?* I could avoid it no longer—it was the moment they'd been waiting for: the greatly anticipated question . . . *How far is too far?*

When I shared the answer the Holy Spirit had given me, the whispering and giggling stopped and you could hear a pin drop. Each girl was visiting this scenario in her mind. *In front of my dad? What would that look like? Come on, we don't do things like that in front of our fathers!*

This is true, for most everything we would do sexually we'd do behind closed doors, in darkened corners, under the cover of night, in a car, or in a drug or alcohol haze. If we were brazen enough, perhaps we'd mess around in a dark room of our homes while our parents slept elsewhere, but never in the light, sober, right in front of our dads!

A hush over the room continued, and I knew it was the right answer to the wrong question from a generation of confused and vulnerable girls. The most alarming revelation for me was the fact I stood before high-school *church* girls under the leadership of a dynamic, passionate, and on-fire youth pastor. I knew the leadership of this youth group hungered for holiness and the fire of God to sweep through the youth and bring with it revival and restoration. I knew these leaders personally pursued purity. Where was the problem? I was soon given some insight.

I preached my message and closed the service at 9 P.M., those who wanted to stay for prayer or just to talk and ask more questions were invited to remain and speak with one of the youth-group leaders or myself. I was shocked at how many girls lingered, their countenances very different from the almost open defiance I'd encountered when I first came in. What I heard for the next two hours broke my heart.

Young girls who trembled under the pain and shame of sexual violation and molestation at the hands of those they'd trusted: friends, boyfriends, uncles, brothers, stepfathers, or even fathers. Young girls tormented by the mental replay of sexually charged images, perverted movies, music videos, photos, or Internet sites. Young girls who felt dirtied by conversations or jokes they'd been part of, overheard, or shamed by names they'd been called. Others were entangled in masturbation.

All these secrets shrouded their young lives like a gray film or clinging residue that refused to be washed off. It lingered behind like the scent of smoke

> ⌐ *They longed to be rescued ... To escape the dark shadows that imprisoned them, but the knights were gone.*

so all might know they'd walked in the midst of unclean fire.

These daughters had no safe haven where they could simply rest and sleep without wrestling images, imaginations, voices, or shadows from their pasts. They were isolated from peace by fear and shame. Some had been equipped with rules but found them to be a faulty protection from the onslaughts waged against their minds. Too often if bodies had escaped physical violation, minds had not. They longed to be rescued by a knight in shining armor. To escape the dark tower of shadows that imprisoned them, but the knights were gone. Too often it was the men in their lives that had disappointed, violated, or abandoned them, leaving them vulnerable and distrustful.

I was told stories of an abuse—so subtle you may mistake it as harmless: parents who watched movies filled with sexual promiscuity, innuendos, and often, partial nudity with their children in the shelter of their homes or beside them in the dark theatre. Young girls shared how uncomfortable they'd been watching this with their parents, especially with their *fathers*. They'd feel shame and fidget, then look at their parents and notice they weren't flinching. After a few such movies or TV shows, they pushed the uncomfortable feelings away, but were unable to see their parents in quite the same light. It was as though by watching their father view the naked breasts of another woman presented in a sexually suggestive manner, their own virgin breasts had been uncovered. They left the experience feeling vulnerable and violated and not even knowing why.

> ⌐ *But how can a daughter feel safe and protected if her father is entertained by promiscuity?*

But how can a daughter feel safe and protected if her father is entertained by promiscuity? Will she sense his protection, disapproval, or disappointment when he is not around if she has not seen it when he is? What happens when little girls no longer feel safe?

Perhaps you have never felt this way, but have found yourself turned off or shut down sexually because of the ugly godless image our society has projected. It would seem the evil one has tarnished the image of healthy desire and love by turning it into a cheap snapshot of lust. Therefore desire and awakening to passion of any kind becomes a frightening prospect. You wonder how you could ever exchange the safety and restriction of the law for the longing and abandonment.

And why, why, *why* would I write a book on the virtues of sexual purity when it appears nobody is really interested or listening? And to whom would I write? In answer, this book is for daughters in waiting. It is for mothers to remember. It is for every fallen one who longs to be lifted. And it is for those who've kept themselves, to know and fully realize their reward and be encouraged to remain strong.

This book is a letter from a generation of mothers and mentors who have known regret, to the daughters of this generation that they might be kept from our failures, and inherit the promises and not the pain. It is a tool for mothers who feel they can't tell their daughters no because years ago they themselves said yes.

This is not a book of do's and dont's . . . it is a book of restoration. A glimpse at how God see things, a revelation of His original intent. Some might call it an impossible fairy tale, but I believe it can be true. Rules will never set us free, just as fear and control will never keep us safe. It is truth that frees us, one that looms larger than all the lies presently surrounding us. Truth is the dawning of morning where there has been a gross and long night of darkness filled with horrible disappointment and despair.

I have heard it said if you want someone to hear something, tell it in a story. I found this to be true many years ago when telling my children stories when they slept in my room. It was a silly, make-believe one set in pioneer days about a family who moved out west and had many adventures. I would tell this story as we were all falling asleep. Often my children would drop in and out of the story as they lapsed in and out of sleep. Along with them I too traveled in and out as I drifted to sleep, and if any of them remained awake they would call me back and correct me if I had left out or messed up on any of the details. I am always amazed because to this day they seem to remember the story with so much more clarity and detail than even I do.

Why have I told you this? Because I believe God wants to tell you a bedtime story, to rock back to sleep what's been

> ∽ *God wants to tell you a bedtime story, to rock back to sleep what's been so rudely awakened.*

so rudely awakened. One to softly lull passions back to a place of waiting and resting in slumber, a story to restore to a dreamlike state what was awakened before its time. A place where fears are calmed and hope is restored. A haven where shame is not permitted, and everything is fresh, new, and clean as flowers after a spring rain.

Before we go there, let's pray together:

∽ *Dear Heavenly Father,*

You are the Creator of heaven and earth. You are the author of intimacy as well. There are areas of my life that have been awakened before the right time . . . areas of my sexuality that hadn't finished resting or dreaming before they were aroused and inflamed. I ask You to touch these places with Your healing rest. As I read, I ask that the light of Your truth would come and dispel the shadows in this area of my life.

I believe You alone can do this, for You are almighty and all-knowing. Open the eyes of my heart that I may know You and walk in Your ways. Let the issues that need to be put to rest be ultimately put to rest. Dispel my fears and draw me under the safety of Your wings. Open my heart and tell me Your stories so I can know and understand Your purpose.

Love,
Your Daughter

2 Where Are We?

In the last chapter, I shared my rude awakening to the reality of where we stand as women and daughters of the Most High God in relation to our sexuality. But how exactly did we arrive at such a desperate and vulnerable state? Was it one wrong step or many that brought us down this path of violation? Did we flirt with those who robbed us of our dignity and then left us naked and powerless? How did the beauty of our feminine forms and the mystery of our sexuality become so cheap and common? How did we move so far from the hope and promise of childhood fairy tales into the shadow and despair of jaded and cynical nightmares?

> ⌒ *How did the beauty of our feminine forms and the mystery of our sexuality become so cheap?*

Dreams give way to nightmares when we heed the whispers and dark lies of the evil one and close our ears and hearts to the voice of Wisdom as she calls aloud to us from the streets (Prov. 1:20). Dreams change to nightmares when we attempt to meet valid needs in invalid and inappropriate ways. Dreams turn into nightmares when heavy yokes, burdens, and cares bend our frames and weigh us down. Dreams yield to nightmares when we allow fear to chase away our hopes and dreams and then paralyze us in our tracks (Josh. 1:9).

I am not interested in giving current facts and figures to pinpoint our literal *statistical* position (such as percentages of divorced families, single moms, or the number of teenagers involved in premarital sex). You can find out such statistics on your own. It is not to your intellect or mind I wish to speak . . . I want to speak directly to your heart. I want to pinpoint our *spiritual* position as women: I believe we're naked and trapped in a nightmare.

Women all over the world are crying out, "I don't like what I see. I want my clothing back! I want my dignity, honor, and mystique restored. I want to push away fear. I want to be empowered and free!"

> ⌒ *I want to pinpoint our spiritual position as women: I believe we're naked and trapped in a nightmare.*

We are living in a nightmare because like disobedient children, we believed the lie that rebellion would set us free. But ultimately it is women who suffer the most when the laws of love are desecrated. This is not a new struggle . . . it is the same one waged in the Garden of Eden long ago when the serpent whispered, *Rebel against God, and you'll be wise and free!* So we took the fruit, ate, and closed our eyes, momentarily reveling in its intoxicating flavor. But when we opened them, we discovered something was amiss. We were naked and

> ⌒ *Ultimately it is women who suffer the most when the laws of love are desecrated.*

covered in shame. We turned to Adam, but he was naked as well and too busy wrestling with his own issues to help or restore us. After all, he was feeling shamed and powerless as well, and blamed us for it!

So the man and the woman run and hide and try to cover their nakedness before God comes into the Garden. With His arrival the blaming begins.

Adam: "The woman you put here with me—she gave me some fruit from the tree, and I ate it" (Gen. 3:12).

Eve: "The serpent deceived me, and I ate" (Gen. 3:13).

God: "And I will put enmity between you and the woman . . . Your desire will be for your husband, and he will rule over you" (Gen. 3:15–16).

Notice Adam blames *both* the woman and God . . . "the woman You put here." What kind of comment is this anyway? What happened to the joyous proclamation of she is "bone of my bones and flesh of my flesh" (Gen. 2:23)? Quite an attitude change has taken place! Something really happened here . . . the two were no longer one, for they were no longer naked and unashamed. Shame had already worked its divisiveness and separated them.

> ⌒ Law demands and dominates, but love leads and gives.

Then the woman is questioned, and she honestly replies, "I was deceived and ate." I don't hear blame in her words, but I do hear remorse and regret. At some level she is already aware of her losses. She will forever be at odds with the serpent. She will desire her husband, but he will rule over her. Here is our first hint the law (the knowledge of good and evil) rather than love is in charge, for law demands and dominates, but love leads and gives.

Too often, like Adam men respond to their own feelings of powerlessness by approaching women as objects to be controlled. They may enforce this control by enacting law in some nations and behaving lawlessly in others. Women are reduced to possessions or sex objects to be conquered, controlled, or used.

And so the wrestling begins. Lost in this struggle for power is the noble origin of women as the completion and helpmeet of man. Lost is the image of a strong and protective male provider. Longing to be restored and whole again, broken and wounded Adams and Eves turn from each other and look elsewhere for their fulfillment. Homosexuality has turned the heads of broken men and risen to prominence by promising them completion through union with other males. But this can never be. When something is complete, it brings forth life; men cannot complete men just as women can never find their completion with other women.

Before the Fall, Adam surveyed all creation in its glorious perfection and found no one who could complete him, that is, until he met Eve. Together, the free man, Adam, and his beautiful counterpart, Eve, would have been invincible, and Satan just could not stand back and watch that happen. So he perverted the pure and perfect truth by questioning God's goodness and wisdom. He deceived Eve into taking the forbidden fruit, and she in turn gave it to the silent Adam at her side. The evil one and father of lies lured them away from God's presence and in the process robbed them of their positions of authority and power.

Then he added insult to their injury by telling each of them the other was the enemy. And the struggle continues between emasculated, angry men and wounded, angry women because each blames the other for their pain and wants them to make it right. But neither men nor women can heal these places . . . only God can restore us again to the garden of our dreams.

The prophesied battle between woman and the serpent still rages (Gen. 3:15). Daughters of God, earthly sons of Adam cannot save you from this serpent . . . it will take a heavenly

> ✑ *Daughters of God, earthly sons of Adam cannot save you from this serpent . . . it will take a heavenly prince.*

prince. The serpent's goal has always been the same: to strip the daughters of Eve of their dignity, strength, and honor and in so doing to render them powerless. In some cultures, he accomplishes this with lawlessness as he encourages them to strip off their clothing and lay bare their beauty for all to see. In other cultures, the serpent enforces laws against her to hide her from the eyes of others by covering her head to toe in garments of shadows. In both cultures, whether she is shrouded or naked, she is covered in shame, and her beauty is paraded as the wicked root of lust and trouble of men.

But when women are stripped of their dignity and degraded, the men are shamed as well, for the woman is the glory of the man (1 Cor. 11:7). When

> ✑ *When women are stripped of their dignity and degraded, the men are shamed as well . . .*

he strips her, he dishonors himself. He loses his God-given desire to protect her and with it his purpose for true authority. Just as we have been stripped of our feminine garments of strength and honor, men have been stripped of their genuine masculine authority.

When femininity and virtue are no longer honored as noble, women are tempted to turn to the lesser powers of seduction and slip on the garments of sensuality. If women never connect with the purpose for their feminine beauty, honor, and dignity, they become incredibly vulnerable to sexual exploitation.

Unfortunately, we have not given our young girls images of females clothed in purity, beauty, and strength. I am not even sure most of us would know what that looked like. Take a look around at the images young women have to choose from. They are bombarded with sexual innuendos before they even develop breasts. Young girls attempt to conform themselves to images of sexually desirable women before they even know what sex is. There are few, if any, attractive and strong images of purity on magazine covers for them to model themselves after, and the choices for older women are no better.

I want you to have the courage to see this struggle for what it really is: You are being stripped of your power, dignity, and clothing by a serpent! You need to see this and be outraged. For only then will you be brave enough to fight your true enemy and give your total allegiance to the faithful and true King. Then you'll find garments to cover your nakedness with splendor. You will wake up and come to the realization it is not men or our husbands we war against, but the enemy of our souls. We must awaken from the nightmare and begin to cry out for the restoration of the dream.

> *⌒ See this struggle for what it really is: You are being stripped of your power, dignity, and clothing by a serpent!*

It is that cry deep in your soul to which I speak . . . that empty, secret place sex cannot fill. You long for a deeper love, intimacy, and communion than a man can bring to you. You long for a safer haven than those found on earth. You cry out for the love of a heavenly Prince. And I have a secret to tell you, whether you believe it or not . . . He longs desperately for you as well. He is the very one who planted this seed of desire deep in the recesses of your heart, and He alone can fulfill your longings.

We will continually be frustrated in our search for fulfillment if we continue to look in all the wrong places. Men are not your problem, nor are they your answer! We need to lift our eyes heavenward, for our help comes from the Lord, the Maker of heaven and earth (Ps. 121:1–2). Only then and there will we find our source and recover our strength and honor.

Why are we as women so vulnerable? We obviously live in a day when lawlessness and iniquity abound

> ⌒ *Men are not your problem, nor are they your answer!*

(Matt. 24:12). When the lawless rule of self reigns, love dies and our protection slips away. When the desire for sin rules the inhabitants of a nation, the delicate balance of the family is upset, and the hearts of women are torn asunder. Desires begin to shift and change, and lies seem to transform to truths. The book of Romans describes this present and accelerating condition in the following verses:

> Therefore God gave them over in the sinful desires of their hearts to sexual impurity for the degrading of their bodies with one another. They exchanged the truth of God for a lie, and worshiped and served created things rather than the Creator—who is forever praised. Amen. (1:24–25)

When we exchange the truth for a lie and serve our own desires rather than the living God, we are degraded and demoted to sexual impurity. When our hearts are set on sexual desire, God lets us have our way. Just as He did not restrain Adam and Eve from their desires in the Garden, He does not now restrain us from our own. He wants to be our true desire, but if we do not long for Him, He lets us have what we want, even if it is harmful to us.

> Because of this, God gave them over to shameful lusts. Even their women exchanged natural relations for unnatural ones. In the same way the men also abandoned natural relations with women and were inflamed with lust for one another. Men committed indecent acts with other men, and received in themselves the due penalty for their perversion. (Rom. 1:26–27)

When pleasure alone and not life giving is the motivation, it is not long before fornication and sexual impurity are no longer enough to satiate our appetites. Desire leads to even more shameful or perverted lusts, and continues on the downward spiral.

> Furthermore, since they did not think it worthwhile to retain the knowledge of God, he gave them over to a depraved mind, to do what ought not to be done. (Rom. 1:28)

When the knowledge of God is rejected, we inherit a state of foolishness and depravity, void of morality or holiness. Here good is lost and we stumble in darkness, tripping from bad to worse. Is it God who's made us depraved? Of course not! His ultimate desire is our restoration, which of course means His ultimate desire is for our hearts to be His. But when we stomp our feet and say, "No! I want what *I* want!" God steps back and lets us have what our foolish willfulness demands.

When men are emasculated, they seek sexual experiences to make them feel masculine again. When men are humiliated, they'll do anything to feel powerful again. In this atmosphere they cry out for fathers and true leadership but too often find none. Without godly examples to follow, in frustration they withdraw from leadership and abandon their wives and children emotionally and far too often physically. Women see the void and try to take the position vacated by the men, but they cannot, and the women and children end up captive. All over the world, emasculated and angry men bully women and children in an attempt to feel empowered again. But it never works.

> *⌒ Punishment has never been God's motivation. He declares freedom!*

Disobedience brings captivity and the sword. But our punishment has never been God's motivation. He wants to declare freedom! Listen to His invitation:

"Come now, let us reason together," says the LORD. "Though your sins are like scarlet, they shall be as white as snow; though they are red as crimson, they shall be like wool. If you are willing and obedient, you will eat the best from the land." (Isa. 1:18–19)

He invites us to be reasonable, to look bravely and truthfully at our condition, and realize it is not a pretty sight! Our sins are not a light shade of pink . . . they are screaming scarlet red and demand a blood sacrifice to appease them. But God doesn't want our crimson sacrifice, for the Prince has already paid the price. God longs to wash us clean. Instead of feeding us empty "food" that doesn't satisfy (sex without intimacy, marriage without covenant), He offers us the best of the land . . . if we will be first willing, and then obedient. Willing to repent and say we've gone astray. Willing to serve Him with joy because He is good, faithful, and true. Willing to submit in obedience to His Word, for it is the law of love, life, and liberty. Willing to take up our cross and hide our life in Christ, the Word made flesh, and follow His example. The words of Joel call to us today:

"Even now," declares the LORD, "return to me with all your heart, with fasting and weeping and mourning." Rend your heart and not your garments. Return to the LORD your God, for he is gracious and compassionate, slow to anger and abounding in love, and he relents from sending calamity. (Joel 2:12–13)

God cries to this generation, *Even now! when everything looks so hopeless, and you feel so dirty and helpless. Even Now! when everyone else has failed, and everything you've tried has disappointed you . . . I will not. Even now! when it looks as though it is already too late . . . it's not! Return to Me with all your heart. The*

> ∽ *The battle has always been for the hearts of women, and God is asking for your broken, bruised, and wounded heart.*

battle has always been for the hearts of women, and God is asking for your broken, bruised, and wounded heart. He is inviting you to turn aside from this present nightmare and step back into His dream, because from the beginning of time He's been searching for a bride . . . just like you.

He calls to captive women everywhere: *Free yourself from these chains and be Mine!* For *"you have stolen my heart, my sister, my bride; you have stolen my heart with one glance of your eyes"* (Song 4:9).

You've stolen His heart . . . now steal away to Him and let Him steal yours. Open your heart to the love and the truth you will find on these pages and let it become alive in you. We have been kissed by this world, and it left us in tears . . . but even now the Prince calls and promises better things for those who respond to His love.

My lover spoke and said to me, "Arise, my darling, my beautiful one, and come with me. See! The winter is past; the rains are over and gone. Flowers appear on the earth; the season of singing has come." (Song 2:10–12)

⌒ *Dear Heavenly Father,*

I hear Your voice calling to me . . . "Even Now!" Steal my heart and keep it safe. Forgive me for embracing lies and turning my back on You. I acknowledge that my sins have been scarlet, and I thank You for the life of Your Son given to make me white as snow. I will count His shed blood as precious. Thank You for waking me up to my true condition. I am tired of being naked, shamed, and afraid . . . I want my clothing back! I turn from images of sensuality and lawlessness, and I embrace again the honor, strength, mystery, and nobility You have hidden in the feminine form. Make Your truth more real than any areas of deception or bondage in my life, so that I might be totally free and completely Yours.

Love,
Your Daughter

3 *Go, and Sin No More*

*I*n the last chapter we spoke of the ancient battle waging between the enemy of our souls, Satan, and the daughters of Eve. He has been constant and persistent in his attempts to shame, strip, and dishonor women from the time of the Garden even until now. Sadly, his most vicious offensive is often launched under the guise of religion. There is nowhere in the Bible where this struggle is more evident than with the woman taken in adultery. It is such an incredible and telling example of the cruelty of law and religion and the beauty of God's mercy and love. I want to visit this scene together with you and perhaps look at it in a very different light.

In the dim light of early morning, we join a large crowd already assembled in the temple court waiting to listen to a young rabbi named Jesus. As women, it is wisest to slip in quietly before the brightness of the sun reveals our presence. Jesus is so different from the other teachers of the law and even condescends to sit among the people when He speaks. There is a gentle strength and a powerful wisdom about this man unlike any other seen or heard. When He speaks, you hear the voice of another unseen . . . in His words you hear the words of the Father God.

Yet controversy follows Him wherever He goes. He speaks so freely of God's love as healing pours out to the sick and afflicted. The religious leaders hate Him, but not the common people . . . they love Him. Women are not supposed to be mixed up with anything controversial. You have been warned to stay away, but you can't. This morning you were irresistibly drawn into His presence. You long to hear again the words He speaks . . . they are the lyrics of a haunting song your heart longs to sing aloud. You wait for Him among this unusually quiet but expectant crowd . . . He has promised to return this morning and teach.

> At dawn he appeared again in the temple courts, where all the people gathered around him, and he sat down to teach them. (John 8:2)

He appears with His disciples at the first gleam of dawn, the sky turning glorious shades of fire as his backdrop. His features are hard to make out with the light of dawn behind Him and the light of morning lingering before Him. After greeting a few in the crowd with hugs, He sits down to teach. You listen with your heart hanging on every word. But there is a disturbance on the horizon.

Over the heads of Jesus and His disciples, you see another group approaching. Their angry voices and dark forms are struggling with someone unseen. As they enter the temple court, you recognize their robes and realize they are the religious leaders. The shape in their midst remains hidden until they are between Jesus and the crowd, then she is thrust at His feet. It is a disheveled woman clutching a remnant of cloth or bedding in an attempt to hide her nakedness, but her covering is not enough. It is obvious she was abruptly dragged from a bed of shame. You wonder where the man is. The leaders are not content to let her cower on the ground; they stand her up for all to see.

> The teachers of the law and the Pharisees brought in a woman caught in adultery. They made her stand before the group and said to Jesus, "Teacher, this woman was caught in the act of adultery. In the Law Moses commanded us to stone such women. Now what do you say?" (John 8:3–5)

What will Jesus say to such a woman? What is to be her fate? Of course, these leaders really don't care about her. They are demanding an answer from Jesus because:

They were using this question as a trap, in order to have a basis for accusing him. (John 8:6a)

Oh, but *you* want His answer. Like every other woman in the crowd that day you need to hear what He will say. What does Jesus say to obviously guilty women? What judgment does He pass on those of which the law demands death? Of course, this woman is a causality of a much bigger plot. It is an

> ∽ *What does Jesus say to obviously guilty women? What judgment does He pass on those of which the law demands death?*

ancient attempt to undermine God, and the real issue is an opportunity for the religious leaders to disqualify Jesus. Watch Him.

But Jesus bent down and started to write on the ground with his finger. (John 8:6b)

At first, He is not willing to look at her or to answer them. He bends down and writes in the dust. The finger of God etches in dust letters that are not recorded for our knowledge. He refuses to turn His eyes to her knowing one so already shamed and frightened could not imagine His glance to be anything but contempt. He will not add His eyes to those now fixed upon her in judgment. Perhaps in His memory He is seeing another who attempted to cover her nakedness in a Garden long ago.

When they kept on questioning him, he straightened up and said to them, "If any one of you is without sin, let him be the first to throw a stone at her." Again he stooped down and wrote on the ground. (John 8:7–8)

The accusing voice of the knowledge of good and evil cries out demanding satisfaction while the King of glory writes in the dust. Maybe in their voices He heard the serpent's accusing voice: *You may cover her, but I will eventually strip and shame again what You cover! She will never learn. She must die at Your hands . . . it is the law!* This time He does not answer the serpent's accusations. It will all be settled soon enough. He speaks only to the accusers now before Him. He asks for the one without sin to throw the first stone and returns to the image in the dust. You hold your breath and wait.

> At this, those who heard began to go away one at a time, the older ones first, until only Jesus was left, with the woman still standing there. (John 8:9)

It would only take one person to release the first stone, and after that all those who took up stones would merely be following another's lead.

> *⌒ Jesus is without sin, but He refused to throw a stone at this woman.*

But no one is present who could throw it . . . or is there Someone? Yes, there is One. Jesus is without sin, but He refused to throw a stone at this woman. He is the only righteous judge, but He had not come to condemn but to save her.

He remains silent until all her accusers are gone. They depart in silence and perhaps in some shame, for they have just admitted to the crowd they'd wanted to trap Jesus in front of their own sinfulness.

Jesus waits until every presence and voice of accusation is gone before He addresses this woman:

> Jesus straightened up and asked her, "Woman, where are they? Has no one condemned you?"
>
> "No one, sir," she said.
>
> "Then neither do I condemn you," Jesus declared. "Go now and leave your life of sin." (John 8:10–11)

Notice she remains until He rises and speaks to her. She is not content to hear His words *about her* she wants Him to *speak to her*. She could have run for cover in the shadows as soon as the last of her accusers left, but she waits . . . naked and ashamed before Him. She is tired of life in the shadows. She stays because she wants forgiveness and release. With

His words she now can leave . . . released from death and openly forgiven, with every question of condemnation removed from her. With these gifts she's empowered to leave her life of sin.

She lifts her head and meets His gaze. In His eyes she sees forgiveness, mercy, and love, and there is something else . . . is it pain? Sensing what has transpired, perhaps another woman from the crowd rises and lays her own garment over this woman's shoulders to cover her nakedness. Perhaps the woman who covers her is you. There is silence as the

> ⌒ *In His eyes she sees forgiveness, mercy, and love, and there is something else . . . is it pain?*

woman walks silently down the very street on which she had just been dragged minutes before. The sun shines brightly, for a new day has dawned for her, one holding renewed hope and promise. Jesus pauses as she departs.

> When Jesus spoke again to the people, he said, "I am the light of the world. Whoever follows me will never walk in darkness, but will have the light of life." (John 8:12)

She is no longer a daughter of death and darkness but of life and light. This was a daughter of Israel, or she would not have fallen under the jurisdiction of the religious leaders. She'd broken covenant and fallen captive to sin. But this unfaithful daughter encountered a merciful Prince, and she was never the same.

A treacherous enemy has dragged the women of this generation naked and guilty before a holy God. Even now, the serpent mocks the Prince with our shame. What is to be done with these daughters of fornication and adultery? Don't they have a covenant with You? Why are they so often found in bed with the world! How many times will You forgive and release them from the judgment of death? It is a heartbreaking question for a heartbroken Prince. For Him there can be only one answer *I do not condemn you. Go . . . and sin no more.* We can be certain He looks at our sin and shame and answer this way because we have the promise of Hebrews 13:8: *Jesus Christ is the same yesterday and today and forever.*

Because of His word and promise, it is time for us to rise up as women and cover our nakedness and the nakedness of others so we might truly go and sin no more. It is time to declare this promise and power to daughters who are still captive to shame.

For the grace of God has been revealed, bringing salvation to all people. And we are instructed to turn from godless living and sinful pleasures. We should live in this evil world with self-control, right conduct, and devotion to God, while we look forward to that wonderful event when the glory of our great God and Savior, Jesus Christ, will be revealed. He gave his life to free us from every kind of sin, to cleanse us, and to make us his very own people, totally committed to doing what is right. (Titus 2:11–14 NLT)

This is great news! Sin no longer has power over us. We can turn from it and say no! Jesus has extended mercy and empowered us with the grace of God. We don't receive the judgment we deserved. We are forgiven and born anew out of death and into life. Beloved daughters, the enemy of your souls doesn't want you to know this. He wants you to remain in shame and therefore bound to sin. He wants to make you think you have no dominion over sin, but that just isn't true. Certainly in our own strength we will try and fail, but we are no longer alone in our battles. We are in Him, and our weapons are mighty!

> *Sin no longer has power over us.*

We are now given freedom and the glorious hope of a future. We have no reason to fear our Lord and Savior's return, for He has redeemed us from wickedness and made us His own. Before, we were eager to do evil . . . now we are eager to do good! When we are truly born again, our natural desires change. He forgives us and then changes our nature with the words, *Go and sin no more.* It is not a prerequisite for forgiveness . . . forgiveness has already been extended. It is a vote of confidence and a belief of better things. Before being born again, fornication and drunkenness were exciting to me. They were what I looked forward to doing in my spare time. I was eager for these activities. But when I was born again, my driving desire to sin left.

The words of Jesus to guilty women like me could be paraphrased this way: "I do not condemn you . . . I forgive and release you from the sentence and judgment of sin. Now go, and sin no more. You are free!" We could never earn the mercy we're extended, just as we could never walk in godliness and say no to sin and worldly passion without the grace of God. Sin no longer has legal claim to our lives. Because . . .

> It is for freedom that Christ has set us free. Stand firm, then, and do not let yourselves be burdened again by a yoke of slavery. (Gal. 5:1)

Stand firm! Stand strong against any condemnation trying to lure you back into a lifestyle of sin. Stand against every shadow of past shame challenging your right to say *no* to ungodliness. Perhaps in the past you had a hard time saying *no* because of guilt and shame, but you are freed from your past and *the past is not your future!* Your future is bright and free!

> Arise, shine, for your light has come, and the glory of the LORD rises upon you. See, darkness covers the earth and thick darkness is over the peoples, but the LORD rises upon you and his glory appears over you. (Isa. 60:1–2)

It is time to step out of the shadows of sin and into His light. Our accusers will silently leave before Him, even now He rises to say, "I do not condemn you. Now go and leave this darkness! I am the light you have been searching for, so sin no more." But we are afraid it is impossible, because we see so much darkness around us. To which He answers, "I know you see darkness on the earth and on its people, but I am your covering of light." Jesus has restored the covering of glory we lost in the Garden.

> ⌒ *Religion cannot cover our nakedness. Men cannot cover our nakedness. Only He can.*

Religion cannot cover our nakedness. Men cannot cover our nakedness. Only He can cover our nakedness with fine linen, bright and clean.

> Then you will look and be radiant, your heart will throb and swell with joy. (Isa. 60:5)

Let's return again to this nameless woman caught in adultery. She is nameless because she could be anyone, for none of us is without sin and too often we bed down with the men, religion, or the world for our affirmation. But these will always disappoint us. Ultimately sin and religion will betray you. Jesus gave dignity, power, and honor to this nameless woman who'd found herself a public spectacle. Jesus looked beyond the obvious and refused to acknowledge her present state as her permanent condition. In essence He told her, "Your past is not your future! Go, and sin no more! Sin was your past, but godliness is your future. Bondage was your past, but freedom is your future. Shame was your past, but dignity is your future. Nakedness was your past, but garments of splendor are your future."

> *⌒ Ultimately sin and religion will betray you.*

Jesus does so much more than forgive this woman . . . He sends her away free. Forgiveness is just the beginning of our freedom, but without the empowerment to move forward, free from the bonds of sin, we'd soon find ourselves ensnared again. We are first lavished with mercy and then strengthened by grace.

> For sin shall not be your master, because you are not under law, but under grace. (Rom. 6:14)

I am afraid for too long grace has not been taught as the power to overcome sin. We have not been brave enough to believe we could ever fulfill Jesus' command to sin no more. We have forgotten that in Him and with Him nothing is impossible, and we have shamed His mercy by preaching grace as a license to sin rather than as a spiritual equipping not to.

Even now the Spirit of the living God, the one called holy, cries to the daughters of this earth:

> Awake, awake, O Zion, clothe yourself with strength. Put on your garments of splendor, O Jerusalem, the holy city. The uncircumcised and defiled will not enter you again. (Isa. 52:1)

Daughters, wake up for the time is shorter than you know. Put on the grace of God and the joy of the Lord, for it is your strength. Over this strength, put on your hope of glory, the garments of splendor. Dream of heaven, and walk as royalty while here on earth, you can dare to hope because you are in covenant, and those outside of covenant, the uncircumcised and defiled, will no longer enter you! No longer will sexual sin and the shame of your past define you . . . you are free! Sin and shame will no longer violate you in the secret places.

> Shake off your dust; rise up, sit enthroned, O Jerusalem. Free yourself from the chains on your neck, O captive Daughter of Zion. (Isa. 52:2)

The Lord says, "Shake off the dust of your past. Stand up unashamed, and take your royal position of authority. I have broken the hold of sin. These chains no longer hold you . . . I do. Remove them from your neck and free yourself, My precious bride!"

We have His grace. It empowers us to free ourselves from the chains around our necks! The power of bondage is broken. The problem has been we believed more in the power of the chains than in the words of our liberator. I challenge you to look not at the chains you

> ⌒ We've believed more in the power of the chains than in the words of our liberator.

see, but at the things unseen, for even now He whispers this invitation and promise to you: *Free yourself from the chains of your past. Their hold on you is not as great as My claim to you. Dare to believe, and throw them off!*

Isaiah 52 is a life Scripture for me. Almost a decade ago, I trembled

> ⌒ *We must know the truth with a greater intimacy than we've known the lie.*

before its promise, mixed it with faith, and found incredible freedom from fear, as I shared in my book *Out of Control and Loving It!* I pass it on to you as a precious promise and gift for the daughters of the Most High in the area of sexual freedom.

It is time for us to know the truth and let it set us free! We must know the truth with a greater intimacy than we've known the lie. To break the power of the lie, I want to expose one that looms very strong in the lives of broken women.

This lie has kept women captive for far too long. It is the reason young women who've compromised themselves sexually at one time feel they no longer have the right to say no. It is the reason the touching of the breast over the shirt gives way to the fondling of naked ones: "I shouldn't have let him touch me to begin with, so how can I say no now?" And of course, the reasoning does not stop there, but continues. It is the same lie that encourages young girls (often virgins) to be pressured to do things that make them feel violated later. They return home, look in the mirror, and see makeup smeared and the freshness and prettiness of a few hours ago gone.

Are some of you crying? Do you remember being shamed in this way and you felt powerless? You were alone with no one to stand up for you. No one yelled, "Enough, leave her alone!" No one protected your honor.

I've found Christian women—young and old—have a hard time saying no because they bear the weight of guilt and shame of previous encounters more heavily than other women do. They believe the lie: Bad girls can't say no. After all, they reason, they've forfeited their rights to purity, dignity, and honor, so they only deserve shame. Intimacy is a forfeited dream, and the best they can hope for is groping in the dark.

But of course, this is a lie. Let's follow the woman caught in adultery. Was she guilty? Yes! Did she deserve judgment? Yes! Was she a captive daughter of Zion trapped in the sin of her past? Yes! But Jesus came to set the captives free. She believed shame was her lot in life, until she heard the words, "go, leave this place, sin no more."

She walks away different . . . she will never be the same again. Her countenance is relaxed, her carriage erect, as she returns by way of the street of shame. As she passes others on the street, they look at her in wonder. They never expected to see her again . . . they presumed her dead under a pile of rocks. It was the law! But of course, something wonderful had happened . . . mercy had triumphed over judgment, and she was forgiven and free to begin her life anew. Actually, she'd lost her life in the presence of Jesus. Instead of stoning her body, He had taken out her heart of stone. This would not be another failed attempt to change. She returned home to bathe and put her clothes on. Sin and shame were no longer her portion, for she had become a trophy of mercy and grace.

I invite you as daughters of the Most High God to turn from the lie and embrace His truth: You are not condemned; you're forgiven. You're free to leave behind sin and shame and go, and sin no more. Let's pray:

⌒ *Dear Heavenly Father,*

My heart quakes at the beauty and the power of Your promise and Your Word to me. I believe Your Word endures forever. I believe You are the same yesterday, today, and forever. This means You look at my sin and shame in all its ugliness, and declare, "I do not condemn you!" I know I deserve judgment, but You have given me mercy. I embrace Your forgiveness and the removal of my garments of sin and shame. I repent of my past and put on Your righteousness, and I stand before You again, naked and unashamed. I receive the grace of God and say a resounding "no!" to ungodliness and worldly passions. I will live self-controlled, upright, and godly in this present age. No longer will I fear Your presence or return. Jesus, You gave Your life to redeem mine from all wickedness and to purify me to be Your very own. I am eager to do good, for sin is no longer my master. You are my Savior and Lord. As I set apart time to read and study, speak tenderly to my heart as only You can. I cast off every chain of bondage and trust my future to you.

Love,
Your Daughter

4 *Awakening Love*

*I*t was late on a beautiful, balmy July evening. I was driving home from a lovely dinner and time of fellowship at a friend's home. Both of our husbands were out of town, and we had enjoyed a casual, spontaneous dinner with our combined total of six children. They had played for hours in the yard while we sat under the stars on her patio and talked until the little ones were quite sleepy. My four sons were quiet as we traveled north back toward our home. Then my oldest son interrupted the silence by pulling an audiotape from his pocket.

"Mom, I want you to hear this song."

There was an immediate chorus of groans and protests from the back seat.

"Not that song again!"

"He's already listened to it twenty times!"

"I don't want to hear that mushy song!"

I was now tipped off to the fact that I was at least not going to be subjected to a heavy bass beat or the loud screaming of some Christian rap group as I had been for the majority of the summer. This promised to be softer and gentler, something I welcomed at this late hour.

"Hey, guys, calm down, I haven't heard it yet, and I want to. Go ahead, put it in," I said.

In response, there were a few more muffled groans from the others, but they were too tired to put up much more of a fight. The tape was slipped in, and I listened intently as a contemporary Christian group sang a very passionate and sentimental love song.

Out of the corner of my eye, I noted that my son knew each word, tone, and inflection of the song. He'd obviously studied it, and as he sang along with such heartfelt tenderness, I found myself becoming slightly uncomfortable. The song proclaimed the power of the artist's undying love and his promise to lay down his life for the object of his love. It was a young man's pledge of his soul in love to a young girl. But something just didn't ring true for me; I have lived long enough to know however noble these sentiments are when they're sung, the follow-through is rare. All this went through my mind in a flash. I realized that my son felt very strongly about this song, so my words needed to be chosen wisely and carefully.

"Isn't that a great song?" he asked in a faraway voice.

"Yes, it is very pretty . . . but what do you think he is promising to do? What does he mean?" I probed.

"He is promising to do anything for his love for her. To prove it even in death if necessary," my son answered.

"Do you think he can keep that promise? It is a beautiful song, but what place has he given this girl in his life? Does she dictate the course he takes, or does God?"

I know you are probably thinking the same thing my son was at the time . . . it's just a love song! It's about time guys promised some kind of commitment. And I agree, but the whole incident got me thinking. Here was my son singing with such passion because deep inside his soul he longs to love someone with that kind of passion, commitment, and noble sacrifice. This song had aroused a desire deep within him that had previously rested dormant, and I knew it.

I looked back over the course of the evening. While all the other children had been playing outside, he had remained inside playing this love song over and over and over again. When he was asked repeatedly to join in their games, he refused. He was captivated by the ideology and

> ⌒ *I saw an awakening . . . and an opportunity.*

beauty of a love so big that he could spend his life in its pursuit and once it was captured, in the protection of its presence.

I saw an awakening . . . and an opportunity.

"You are at the age when love begins to awaken. You have a choice to make. You can allow romantic love to awaken and be frustrated for

> ⌒ *You can allow romantic love to awaken and be frustrated or you can purpose to awaken another type of love, your passion for God.*

the next five to eight years until you find the girl you'll marry. Or you can purpose to awaken another type of love, your passion for God. You must choose between these two types of love, for the time has come for one or the other to awaken."

Solomon knew and understood this and penned a charge to youth that would stand for all time:

Remember your Creator in the days of your youth, before the days of trouble come and the years approach when you will say, "I find no pleasure in them." (Eccl. 12:1)

That night, I shared with him in a simpler form what I now share with you. It is in our youth that love awakens and our heart is directed. It is supposed to. But we must actively control and determine which type of love arises and begins to dictate our actions. We must allow romantic love to rest and dream until the time of its awakening so natural passion will remain dormant, but at the same time we must arouse a passionate love for God. Can we love intensely in one area while remaining consciously passive in another? I believe we can. It is accomplished in the same manner we'd awaken natural romantic love in the first place but with a different focus.

To explain how this is possible, I'm going to go way back and draw on my first encounters with romantic or puppy love from grade school. This was definitely a prelude to my high-school years, but up until about the fifth grade I really had no interest in boys. They were merely the creatures that annoyed my best friend, Marci, and I as we talked on the playground or walked to school. We often held hands while we bared the deepest secrets of our souls to each other, that is, until some wild boy would come barreling down upon us and break the bond of our grip and steal one of our hats in the process. (Usually Marci's because she was the prettiest.) This of course meant war! We would run after them and demand the return of our stolen property, all the while threatening them in every imaginable way and calling them an extensive and impressive list of names. We were died-in-the-wool tomboys and refused to stand for bullying from some irritating *boys!*

At some point in the process, the boys would back down and realize we were truly tough, the hat would be returned, and we would run the rest of

> ⌐ *It is in our youth that love awakens and our hearts are directed.*

the way home laughing and shouting, arms raised in triumph. But after the fourth grade, Marci moved away, and I was left to fight the boys alone.

In fifth grade things began to change. I started getting notes from boys asking me for my "list." In case you are not aware, the "list" was a ranking of boys I liked in descending order. At first I was a little slow and would not participate with the list-ranking escapades. But then I started hearing things that intrigued and interested me such as:

"Lisa, you're number three on Stuart's list, and you're number two on Ricky's."

I always answered back, "I don't want to be on their stupid lists!"

But I began to think . . . if I was number two or three, then who was number one? I mean, just because I didn't like them didn't mean I didn't want to be first on their lists! Wasn't I one of the fastest runners in the class? Surely that had to count for something! I had to be number one on someone's list . . . the question was, whose?

Then I began to notice the list had a power of its own. Girls I thought of as boring, Barbie-doll players were outranking me on the lists of boys with whom I played kick the can, all because they had granted those hat stealers high ranking on their lists. Maybe I would have to make a list of my own, or maybe I would go for broke and name only one boy. I did kind of like this one guy. He was the only one who came to mind when I was pushed for an answer at slumber parties. You know, the ultimate question, "I know you don't like anyone, but if you *had* to marry someone (like if you were at gunpoint), who would you pick?"

He was smart, popular, and cute . . . all the girls liked him, so I never wanted to say his name because I was sure they would all laugh at me. (Remember, I was an avowed tomboy.) So I always said "No one! I'm not ever getting married!"

But when I lay down in my sleeping bag at the slumber parties, he was the one on my mind, and things were changing between us. He teased me a lot on the playground and in class. But when we were seated next to each other in Social Studies, he was always talking to me. We even passed deep and sensitive notes like: "Do you think this class is cool or dumb? (Check one.)" After a while I started hearing rumors that I was climbing the ranks of his list, but I remained quiet.

Then one day in class he sent *the* note. He was serious, and he wanted to know who was first on my list. (My list, which still did not exist!) Without answering, I turned the note over and asked him who was first on his. He crumpled my reply and sent a new scrap of paper declaring: "I asked you first." I sent it back, with a defiant: "So? I asked you second!" There was no way I was going to say he was first on mine and have him rank me second! I figured if he put me first I would put him first, but if he put me second, I'd demote him to second place as well. All of a sudden, my thoughts were interrupted by the teacher, who was calling out both our names and warning us to stop passing notes or she'd read them aloud to the class! We both blushed and looked down for a long time.

Then he whispered, "Write the person's name on the bottom of your shoe, and I'll write it on mine, and we'll both show it to each other at the same time."

"Okay," I agreed, but I was going to trick him. Instead of writing a name, I wrote another word. I was too afraid my name would not appear on his shoe sole.

"I'll count to three, and then we'll show it, okay?" he said.

I nodded, smiling and trying to act cool when all the while my ten-year-old heart was racing out of control.

"One, two, three." He whispered as he presented his shoe sole for my inspection. On it were the initials *P. B.*, which was his nickname for me. I was a little slower raising my foot with the block letters *BURN* on it. Needless to say, he was not happy, and I immediately fell out of favor and dropped completely off his list. We both turned red, and he wouldn't speak to or even look at me for the rest of class. Now that I knew I'd blown it, I realized I liked him for sure! But he wasn't going there with me again. And there was another problem . . . there was a new boy at our school named John (not my husband), and he was telling everyone I was first on his list. All the girls liked him because he was new, but I didn't like him. I liked the one who'd gotten away.

The more I heard that John liked me, the more I protested his attention. After all, he wasn't even in my class. I only saw him on the playground and when we passed in the hall during the changing of classes. I would turn my face the other way and refuse to receive any note he tried to pass me. Then one day he pushed me too far.

I was walking home with a few friends and this John and his friend Eric were following closely behind us on their bikes, making comments in an annoying singsong way, something like, "John likes Lisa, John likes Lisa." I was desperately trying to ignore them, but now my friends were giggling and joining in the song as well. My face was getting hotter and hotter. I turned around to give the guys my meanest dirty look and raise a threatening hand their way when John rushed me, stole my hat, and took off on his bike. I ran after him with all my might and caught up to him at a tree. He'd dropped his bike and put the tree trunk between us while waving my hat to taunt me.

"Who do you like? Tell me, and I'll give you your hat back," he demanded.

I had just about had it. How dare he take my hat and order me around? I picked up a large stick that I found at my feet (well, actually it was a small log), and waved it threateningly at him while yelling:

"You give me back my hat, or I'll hit your bike!"

He was unfazed. "Go ahead! Hit my bike. I don't care because . . . I love you!"

What?! Had he said "love"? Now everyone was laughing, and I was furious. He was ruining everything! Before I knew what was happening, I had leaped around the tree trunk and was within log's reach of him. I demanded the return of my hat once more, but instead of handing it over, he repeated his profession of love. That did it. I'd had enough humilia-

> ⌒ That did it. I'd had enough humiliation . . . I raised the big stick and hit him over the head with it .

tion . . . I raised the big stick and hit him over the head with it. He dropped the hat, I dropped the log, my friends all gasped, and his friend came running to his side. Without checking to see if he was okay, I snatched my hat back, pulled it firmly down on my head, grabbed the hands of my friends, and began the long march home.

My face was hot and flushed. My friends were not sure what to think. Was John a love hero? Was I terrible? I was adamant in the defense of my behavior. I'd warned him . . . he hadn't listened. Now maybe he'd leave me alone! I entered my home and ran back to my room after telling my mom that the annoying boy named John had taken my hat! I even vowed never to marry anyone named John in protest of his behavior. (Never say never!) In the safety of my room, I recovered myself and started my homework. Time passed, and the doorbell rang. From my bedroom window, I could see the front porch, and on it was a woman I knew to be John's mother.

My stomach sank because at some level I knew I was in trouble. I sneaked down the hall a ways so I could hear what was being said at the door. The story went something like: "Our son told your daughter he liked her, and she hit him on the head with a log." I almost yelled in protest, but I heard my mother say, "Well, I understand he took her hat." The muffled voice said something about blood and stitches, and my mother began apologizing. How could she?! More muffled voices followed, and in them was the assurance I would be spoken to, and then the mother of the enemy left.

After closing the door, my mother went to the family room to tell my father the whole ugly story. I listened carefully for yelling, but instead I heard laughter. They were remarking about my behavior. I slithered back to my room just in time, for they were now heading my way for the big talk. They did their best to explain to me the seriousness of hitting someone in the head with a log, whether prewarned or not. They told me I could have killed him, but I had just split open his scalp, and he had gotten a few stitches. I was feeling a little foolish, knowing this meant there would be a bandage for all to see the next day. Everyone would know I'd hit the new boy.

"He must really like you," my mom said as she left my room closing the door behind her.

But I wondered would he, could he, possibly still like me after being hit in the head and getting stitches? Perhaps the other boy would see it as a proclamation of my liking him. Or maybe he would just be afraid of me now! I went to bed wondering what the next day would bring and feeling a little silly and out of step.

The next morning, my classroom was abuzz, and my teacher gave me a knowing look when I walked in.

"Is it true you hit John and busted open his head?" the group clustering around me asked.

"Yes," I answered, trying to be nonchalant as though to tell them to stop making a big deal out of this.

From her desk a Barbie-doll player spoke up, "I can't believe you're *still* first on his list."

I knew he was first on hers. This little blonde had a major crush on him. I couldn't believe I was still even on the list! Wow! My mom was right . . . he must really have liked me. That day I decided to leak the rumor that I was *thinking* about liking him and adding him to my list. (After all, it was the least I could do after wounding him so badly!) I even took the note he slipped me in the hall that day. But truthfully, I was intrigued by his persistence. This sweet fifth grader named John stayed true to me until he moved away the following summer. (He cried when he left.) He came over almost nightly, and we stood on my front porch and talked. I don't believe I ever hit him again, and as you all know . . . I did end up with a John. After all, how could I resist such a stubborn, safe love? Good question. How could any of us?

> We love *because* he first loved us. (1 John 4:19, emphasis added)

We can love because God first loves us, making us feel safe. He is faithful, and we are all *first* on His list. This is not some fleeting, elementary-school crush or a middle-school puppy love that fluctuates with every changing semester or when threatened with the appearance of a new girl. We have an assurance of His

> ⁓ *We have an assurance of His love because He loved us before we even glanced His way.*

love because He loved us before we even glanced His way. He even went as far as to record it in a book for all to see, not just scrawling it on some piece of scrap paper that eventually is thrown away. He declares His love to be everlasting, and He backs it with the promise of covenant.

> "I have loved you with an everlasting love; *I have drawn you* with loving-kindness." (Jer. 31:3, emphasis added)

Notice God uses past-tense terms here. He says, "I have loved" as though to say, *I decided a long time ago to love you, and it is never going to change. Therefore I have reached out and done everything within My power to draw you to Me. To capture your attention, I've spared no loving-kindness so you would know it is settled with Me.*

Therefore, our first step in awakening our love for God is to *realize* and *acknowledge* His love for us. We must have the revelation that even though our behavior was unattractive and repulsive, He pressed near our angry, log-waving forms and whispered in our ears, "I love you." We take the note as from His hand. We read it and allow the weight of its truth to sink into our hearts. We look

> ⌒ *No, not there, my child; your name is written on the palm of My hand.*

for our names on the bottom of His shoe, but He lifts our gazes to show us, *No, not there, my child; your name is written on the palm of My hand.* And then He opens it to reveal the wound that etched our names indelibly on His palm.

> Or do you show contempt for the riches of his kindness, tolerance and patience, not realizing that God's kindness leads you toward repentance? (Rom. 2:4)

Once we are confronted with this truth so beautiful and immense, we have another choice. How will we respond to this realization? Will we receive His embrace and respond in turn, or turn away from the touch of the unseen to have contact with those we can see and touch?

I will admit this is honestly not an easy crossroad, but it is one each of must stand at and decide, regardless of our age or relationships. As Christians and disciples of Christ, we know the way we should choose, but knowing *how* to walk that path is not always immediately clear. For the promise of immediate gratification initially looks better than treasured hope with the delay of longing.

Our second step in awakening our passion for God is to respond to His advances and move beyond the acknowledgment of His love for us by choosing to pursue Him. We turn our faces toward Him that we might know as we are known.

But how do we respond to One we cannot see? He is the Prince of promise, and cannot yet be seen or touched. It is as though we fell asleep in the warm sunshine of a flower-filled glen and awoke to find a beautiful, handwritten note declaring the undying love of the Prince of the universe written in His own hand. The letter not only declares His love, but in it He offers us a covenant of marriage. We are overjoyed as we hold the letter in our shaking hands and examine the royal emblem beside His name. We jump to our feet, heart racing . . . where is this gracious Prince who loves me? I must know Him . . . I must see His face. We look all around, but He is nowhere in sight.

What would you do? I think you'd begin looking for Him. I think you would even ask others about His whereabouts.

> All night long on my bed I looked for the one my heart loves;
> I looked for him but did not find him.
> I will get up now and go about the city, through its streets and squares; I will search for the one my heart loves. (Song 3:1–2)

Suddenly our eyes would lift from our small world of self, and we would take a fresh look around us. We would stare deeply into each sunrise and sunset trying to catch a glimpse of Him. In it we would glimpse His goodness, and that goodness would become ours. We'd stare in wonder at the stars of the heavens reveling in the awe of His majesty, and in turn, a portion of their brilliance would rain down upon us.

We'd stand in a new wonder at the splendor of the creation looming all around us, for now we are not just creatures moving about on the face of the earth. The realization of His love changes all that. It has now become personal, for we are His and He is ours. Each day becomes a gift, every flower personally sent. We would receive every good thing as from His hand, we'd take it all in and hold it close to our hearts, letting it love us with its loveliness.

> For since the creation of the world God's invisible qualities—his eternal power and divine nature—have been clearly seen, being understood from what has been made. (Rom. 1:20)

Now we respond differently to our surroundings, for we see in the visible beauty around us His invisible qualities or nature. We observe His personality in every detail, large and small. Because we are loved, we now watch for Him. It is not unlike me with my silly, fifth-grade beau . . . instead of turning away from him in the halls, I watched for him. I anxiously read every note he wrote and transferred them to my secret drawer at home. I reread them later in the personal atmosphere of my room with love songs playing in the background. After school I'd slow down and trail behind my friends so he could catch up and walk me home. I was looking for opportunities to spend time with him, and so should we look for opportunities to be with our Prince.

Music becomes a haven for blossoming love. There is a beautiful and divine connection between love and music. They expand and reveal each other. Music has the power to transport us. Love soars on the wings of music and awakens a song in our hearts. Words immersed in music can touch places in our hearts that nothing else can reach. All of us have found ourselves swept into an ecstasy of great joy or lowered into the depths of sorrow by the power of a song.

> ⌒ *There is a beautiful and divine connection between love and music. They expand and reveal each other.*

Music is an essential key to the awakening of our love for God, because music has the power to usher us past our present reality and into the very presence of God. It lifts our truest and deepest emotions closer to the surface and transports us to a dimension closer to the heart of God. The influence music has on us intensifies as we enter adolescence. He can speak for us when words are hard to express and our feelings are so overwhelming. As a youth David used the power of music to draw him closer to God and keep loneliness at bay while tending sheep. As He sang He sensed God's presence with him in the wilderness. Later, when king, he described the relationship between music and God this way:

But You are holy, enthroned in the praises of Israel. (Ps. 22:3 NKJV)

Our praises exalt the position, power, and authority of God in our lives. Again, it is noteworthy that most of us find ourselves more keenly aware of music's effect on us during our adolescence. We are drawn almost irresistibly to it in the same season of our lives when love is awakening.

> ⌒ *Our praises exalt the position, power, and authority of God in our lives.*

It comes at the time when we are the most emotionally vulnerable, for music has the power to comfort or enflame.

Do you know there is an anointing on music? Therefore you must choose it wisely. What do I mean by an anointing? In the Old Testament, the anointing was most often associated with the pouring forth of oil on a king, priest, or prophet. It was a tangible representation of God's Spirit. In the New Testament, the anointing represented the indwelling and empowerment of the Holy Spirit to reveal Christ. So godly, anointed music is empowered by the Spirit to draw us into His presence. There have been times of worship when I've been utterly overcome by His presence. Though I did not see Him with my eyes, it was as though he encompassed my entire being. In that presence, I feel completely safe and loved. Time stops, and I glimpse heaven. I always leave these encounters with a greater love and a deeper hunger for God. Spirit-breathed, life-giving music has the power to heal, inspire, and quiet our souls. When I hear the song again, whether it is years or days later, the memory of the encounter makes the past become the present.

Therefore music has the power to build memories. When John and I were newly married, he swept me away to St. Martin. There we rested and caught up with each other over long meals and on moonlit balconies. There was an instrumental song we heard over and over in our hotel restaurant, and now eighteen years later, when I hear its first notes, I am swept back to that place and time. In a moment I am in a candlelit restaurant called Waves overlooking a glistening ocean under a starry sky, and I'm speaking softly with my husband.

Music has the power to take you places emotionally. Because of this it is important we choose our destinations wisely. There is music that makes us weep with patriotic pride. We have all felt this at one time or another when singing our national anthem; usually its effect is most keenly felt in times of national hardship or victory. There is music that brings heaviness and despair, encouraging hopelessness, death, or even suicide. Other songs incite anger, hatred, and rebellion. I don't believe anyone would argue about the power and influence of music in these areas.

Music has the power to arouse and awaken romantic feelings as well. It has the ability to stimulate unconscious sexual responses in the human body. Various beats drive the physical body to a heightened state of arousal, and when this is accompanied by sexually charged lyrics, the influence of this combination is undeniable.

If you desire to walk in purity, you must guard against the influence of this type of music, it will bypass your first line of defense and take up residence in your mind . . . even if you don't want it to. You might never have personally sung the lyrics, but there it is anyway, repeating its message over and over in your head. We've all heard people complain, "I have that stupid song stuck in my mind!"

The best method to rid yourself of songs that bear messages you don't want reinforced is to displace them by singing or listening to another. There are the

> ⌒ *Worship always empowers the worshiper with a greater revelation of the object of her desire.*

songs of earth, and there are the songs of heaven. Not all songs of earth are bad, but most will not draw you closer to God, but the songs of heaven will. When we sing these songs we proclaim our love and desire for God. This is a form of worship, and worship always empowers the worshiper with a greater revelation of the object of her desire. Never in the history of time has there been more Spirit-breathed, transforming music available. Use it to bask in God's presence . . . it cannot help but draw you closer to Him, because music was always meant to draw lovers closer.

In summary, one way to awaken, strengthen, and nourish your love for God is to model the same approach you'd use to awaken romantic love, create atmosphere with song. You draw closer to God by listening to and singing love songs to and about Him. Paul described being filled with the Spirit this way:

> Be filled with the Spirit. Speak to one another with psalms, hymns and spiritual songs. Sing and make music in your heart to the Lord. (Eph.5:18–19)

In this verse, we find an admonishment to be filled with the Spirit. We are filled as we sing out loud and make music in our hearts, but this verse introduces another key as well . . . our communication about God with others. This is not talking about some sterile form of witnessing, because too often we can get hung up on that as a form of works. No, this is a conversation born out of love, words that pour forth from a heart that's overflowing. Remember, it is exciting to be loved, and you will want to share the beauty of it with others.

When you love someone, you rehearse their attributes for others. You brag about your involvement with them. When the friends share a common love of something, then there is a common bond of passion. This shared passion could be likened to a circle of friends standing about a campfire, all freely enjoying its warmth and beauty while its light dispels the surrounding darkness and keeps wild animals at bay. There is a bond that causes each of you to build up the others and strengthen one another in truth. Another way to further awaken and strengthen your love for God is to surround yourself with friends who speak well of Him.

Be assured that if you choose to awaken a passion for God rather than a passion for the opposite sex, you will have to choose your friends wisely. You will have the freedom to be much more careless if you pursue common, earthbound love at this point in your life.

> ⁓ *If you choose to awaken a passion for God, you will have to choose your friends wisely.*

But if you choose to chase the dream of a Prince, you're going to have to surround yourself with other ladies in waiting. I know this is easier said than done, but they are out there. True friends of Christ will be true friends to you. They'll speak well because they live well.

You are my friends if you do what I command. (John 15:14)

Jesus is clear here. Friends of Jesus keep His commands and encourage others to do the same. True friends will always lift you higher and chal-lenge you to walk in a manner pleas-ing to our Lord. When your friends

> ⌐ *True friends will always lift you higher and challenge you to walk in a manner pleasing to our Lord.*

follow Jesus, you're all heading the same direction, and share a common road map. This principle is true whether you are young or old . . . true friends provoke you to good works.

As iron sharpens iron, a friend sharpens a friend. (Prov. 27:17 NLT)

Surrounding yourself with those who are one in spirit and purpose is crucial. This does not mean you will always agree on everything, but because you all have fellowship with the Spirit you should each remain teachable and protective of one another.

Above all else, guard your heart, for it is the wellspring of life. (Prov. 4:23, emphasis added)

Our heart is to be given the top priority. If a thief came into your room and stole everything of material value, he'd really have nothing because he could not touch your heart. The only way a heart can be stolen is if you have somehow attached it to something else. Then your loss could be truly great. This is the reason God tells us to love Him with our entire hearts because in Him our hearts are kept safe. Another rea-son we are to guard our hearts is that springs of life come from them. Another Bible version tells it this way:

Above all else, guard your affections. For they influence everything else in your life. (Prov. 4:23 TLB)

Another description of the heart is our "affections." *The location of your affections will drive the direction of your decisions.* Your affections will ultimately influence every area of your life. In this chapter, we're talking about awakening our passion and love for God, and this involves setting our hearts on Him. Again the question becomes, how do I set my heart on a God I cannot see?

> ⌒ *The location of your affections will drive the direction of your decisions.*

If you want to know how to do something, you counsel with someone who has already learned to do it well. King David knew how to pursue God and maintain a passion for Him. He pressed into God like no other man before him. He began this quest in his youth and was still pursuing God when he was an old man. David never doubted God's love or faithfulness and lived his life in constant response and thanksgiving to Him.

Keep me safe, O God, for in you I take refuge. I said to the LORD, "You are my Lord; apart from you I have no good thing." . . . I have set the LORD always before me. Because he is at my right hand, I will not be shaken. Therefore my heart is glad and my tongue rejoices; my body also will rest secure. (Ps. 16:1–2, 8–9)

What is David doing? He is setting the Lord before him. How is he doing it? By bringing forth the declarations of his heart by the words of his mouth. You set your unseen heart with your words, for our hearts are always revealed by the words we speak. Conversely, the heart is transformed by the words we speak as well. Not only did David tell us what he did, he gave us the very words he used so we can make these declarations. In this psalm, David brings out some powerful truths here that we need to make our own:

1. Even kings cannot protect themselves . . . make God your refuge.

2. Call Him yours, your Lord . . . make it personal.

3. Tell Him there is nothing you desire more than Him.

4. Set Him permanently before you.

5. Give Him preeminence, and honor Him with your life.

6. Follow Him in everything you do.

7. Because He's in charge, you will stand.

8. Since you're no longer in charge, relax and rejoice.

9. Rest in Him.

When you speak declarations of love and covenant with God, you strengthen the bonds between you. He is already completely committed to you, but you can increase your commitment to Him. The very process by which salvation comes into our lives is how we continue our romances with God.

> *When you speak declarations of love and covenant with God, you strengthen the bonds between you.*

> If you confess with your mouth, "Jesus is Lord," and believe in your heart that God raised him from the dead, you will be saved. For it is with your heart that you believe and are justified, and it is with your mouth that you confess and are saved. As the Scripture says, "Anyone who trusts in him will never be put to shame." (Rom. 10:9–11)

We enter into and expand every relationship in our lives through words and corresponding actions. These may be words that declare commitment such as vows, oaths, or pledges. Or these may be less formal but nevertheless powerful words spoken between family and friends. Words draw us closer in their revelation of our dreams and fears in a safe and loving environment. Words can bring healing and cleansing to the secret places of our lives just as surely as they can wound and defile our innermost beings.

To guard the passion and presence of God in your heart, choose your words the way you choose your friends . . . wisely. Know they will be few but precious.

This may not be a revelation to you, but most of us are innately selfish. This means that in our humanity we do not know how to love well. God is asking for all of our imperfect love, and in exchange He will give us His perfect love. He will even empower us to love Him. He promises to *pour out his love into our hearts by the Holy Spirit, whom he has given us* (Rom. 5:5). We need only to ask Him.

⌒ Dear Heavenly Father,

I feel the stirring. I cry out for my love for You to awaken in response to Your love. I was faithless when You were ever faithful. I want to know You. Reveal Yourself. I press in and pray the words of David, for my heart runs after You. Keep me safe, O God, for in You alone I will take refuge. You are my Lord, and apart from You I have no good thing. I hide my heart in Your secure treasury. I set You always before me. Because You walk at my right hand, I will not be shaken. I believe this, and my heart is glad. I will sing aloud and praise You with my heart and my soul. I will lie down and rest, secure and safe from harm, for I am in Your shelter, and under Your wing I hide.

Love,

Your Daughter

5 Sleeping Beauty

A dream is a wish your heart makes when it's fast asleep.

—FROM CINDERELLA

We sing and tell stories with our lips that betray the longings of our hearts. Perhaps the title of this chapter took you by surprise, but it shouldn't, for it was God who originally came up with this concept. After all, He is the only King of the universe and His Son, Jesus, the original crown Prince, is the ultimate redeemer of all captive beauties. This is but one of His many love stories, and good love stories have gardens and castles, thorns and fruit, gates and towers, forests and field, good and evil, glorious princes and sleeping beauties.

> ⌒ *He is the only King of the universe and His Son, Jesus, the original crown Prince, is the ultimate redeemer of all captive beauties.*

This story in its simplest form relates the plight of a captive daughter waiting to be awakened. If you will delve a little deeper with me into this tale, you will find it possesses an amazing depth and range of emotion, including our darkest fears and our most desperate dreams. This ancient fairy tale calls to men and women alike, for it is but a glimpse, a lifting of the curtain from our limited earthly perspectives into the mystery and splendor of heaven's most enduring promises. It captures in the simplicity of childlike words the deepest and dearest desire of every woman . . . that she might awaken from a passing nightmare and find herself forever transported into a dream.

> ◟ *It captures in the simplicity of childlike words the deepest and dearest desire of every woman . . . that she might awaken from a passing nightmare and find herself forever transported into a dream.*

This hope stirs the hearts of young girls and old women alike. Imagine what it would be like to be rescued by a love bigger and stronger than any of our chains, a love capable of navigating the deep emotional moats surrounding your life. It is a love brave enough to face off any dragon threatening your heart. This rescue would include an escape from dark fortresses of our own construction, for far too often we are the architects of our own demise. It would break through the isolation of walls we have built to keep others at bay. How remarkable to discover that while we waited in dark slumber, a lover, noble beyond compare, fought through every barrier with the burning desire to awaken us with a kiss. Please indulge me as I take some creative liberties and look for our Prince in this story.

Though there are many versions of this tale, most open with a banquet where a king and queen are celebrating the long-awaited birth of their only daughter with a royal feast. In their excitement and haste, these parents inadvertently offended an evil fairy by neglecting to invite her. Even though the fairy was scorned, she attended the banquet anyway, and while the other guests gave gifts to bless the newborn infant, she bestowed a curse. The effect of this curse was not immediate . . . it waited, lurking in the shadows of tomorrow, promising to ensnare their daughter as she made the transition from girlhood to womanhood. According to the curse, on her fifteenth birthday she would hastily reach for a spindle on a spinning wheel, prick her finger, and fall dead.

Another fairy in attendance interceded for the girl and reduced the death to a lengthy sleep. The king and queen were horrified and reacted by immediately passing laws to protect their daughter. They burned every known spindle and spinning wheel in their kingdom and outlawed the production of more.

> ◟ *Delayed curses are the most perilous, for as time passes by, they lose some of their immediate edge.*

But delayed curses are the most perilous, for as time passes by, they lose some of their immediate edge. In the fairy tale, fifteen years passed, and the king and queen became confident, with all spindles destroyed long ago, their daughter was safe.

I wonder what would have happened if, instead of rashly destroying the spinning wheels and passing laws against their use, the king and queen had taken the time to carefully instruct their daughter in how to properly handle one. After all, spinning wheels are not bad . . . they're good. What if this daughter had become skillful and proficient at spinning? There would never have been any reason to fear her hastily grasping at a spindle, for she would have known to handle it carefully.

What then? Of course, things would have been very different, and what had been forbidden would have lost its appeal and intrigue. But they did not do this because, like most parents, they listened to fear . . . and fear is never a wise or good counselor to us. When fear directs our decisions it always deals in extremes rather than in wisdom and moderation. Too often we take the same measures today. But let's return to our story.

The daughter grew up to be beautiful, intelligent, and charming, and her parents were certain she would be as obedient in their absence as they had known her to be in their presence. With this false assurance, they became careless and failed to search the remote rooms of their castle for spindles. On their daughter's fifteenth birthday, they accepted an invitation to enjoy the hospitality of another king. As they left behind their daughter, they charged her to be good and remain within the castle grounds, promising a quick return.

But this daughter had never known such freedom, and she could not wait to explore the palace and search out the very tower her parents had neglected to secure. As their carriage slipped from sight, her heart soared with excitement. Today would be an adventure, for she would find out what is behind the doors of every hidden room! Of course, it was not long before she opened one to find an old woman busy spinning thread on a spinning wheel. The princess was intrigued . . . she had never seen such an instrument before. She watched as the wheel turned round and round, and fluffy cloudlike wool was captured and spun tightly into taut, strong thread. Its draw was irresistible, and the old woman motioned the princess closer.

She stepped nearer and then stretched forth her hand. The old woman nodded her approval, whispering, "Go ahead, touch it . . . take the spindle." She did, and pricked her finger, drawing blood. She pulled back her hand, but it was too late, and she began to feel strangely faint. The old woman smiled and motioned her to a bed waiting in the shadows. It was shrouded and dark, but she was too tired to protest. She sank into its folds to avoid dropping onto the wooden floor. Sleep rolled over her like a wave, and as she was overcome, she heard the mocking laughter of an old, scorned woman. Darkness enfolded her castle home, and thorns and briers quickly overgrew and obscured the castle from the view of any outsiders.

Many, many years passed, and the story of this sleeping beauty was told in the court of the most handsome, brave, and noble of all princes. Her captivity had become so ancient the bearers of her tale were not even certain if the words they recited were true or mythical legend. But the prince knew. He was so moved by the desperation of her plight he immediately withdrew from the pleasures of his court to make ready his departure, for he would go and rescue the princess. He would leave on his quest the following morning. There was an urgency . . . it was her time to awaken.

His journey took him far from his homeland, and after many days, he entered the dark borders of her distant country. But he was not welcomed there. Finally, an old woman shared with him the story she heard as a child from her mother, the legend of a lonely princess lost deep in a dark forest on the other side of the vast, arid wilderness that surrounded their city. He thanked her and began the lonely crossing of this ancient desert.

It was a long, hard journey, and his supplies did not match its length. He was repeatedly tempted with discouragement by an evil adversary who first offered food and then the throne of his dark kingdom if the prince would turn back from his quest, but the prince pressed on. Nothing he was offered could alter his desire to share the glory of his father's kingdom with this caged daughter.

He reached the forest to discover it was a dense tangle of underbrush and tree growth. After many days he hacked his way through the thorny sentinels and came upon the castle. Vines of steel had scaled the ramparts and entwined the towers, disfiguring its appearance until it was no longer a thing of beauty, but a living monstrosity. Only one lone tower had managed to remain above the reach of the thorns. The prince knew in this tower she waited for him.

He listened in the ominous stillness that hovered over the structure of thorns. The dwelling seemed to sneer, Go! You can never reach her . . . she's mine, but he imagined he heard another voice. It was her whisper, faintly bidding him to come. He was her last hope. With renewed strength, the prince wielded his powerful sword and hacked through the thorns barring his entrance. With every blow, he was closer to waking her and making her his own. He kicked open the door.

Inside, the air was still and stale and thick with dust. He mounted the winding staircase to her tower chamber, passed through the door, opened the window, and with one motion dispelled the darkness. Golden light spilled onto her sleeping figure. While she waited, she had neither soiled nor aged; her time of waiting had served her well, and she had become more beautiful in her rest.

The prince walked closer, still breathing hard from the battle. But when he paused a moment to look at her in rest, she was breathtaking. The prince was so moved he wept. Propelled by a desire that had grown deeper with his journey, he embraced her tenderly. His warm lips rested momentarily on her lifeless ones, and then he straightened himself and watched for her response.

Her eyes began to flutter under heavy lids, and then they slowly opened as her head turned. She saw her prince and smiled a sweet, sleepy smile as she lifted her hand to his tear-stained cheek. When her fingers touched the trail of his tears, her own began. She was face-to-face with the very one of whom she had dreamed. The one she'd never seen but always known. At last, it was He! There was no turning back for either of them; she had captured His heart with just one glance. He took the hand resting upon His cheek and kissed it passionately.

Then in one move, He lifted her from her shadowy prison of darkness and carried her out into the now-brilliant sunlight where His white horse was waiting. There was no talk of the evil spell or fading palace. All that was before was gone; the past was but a shadow fleeing at the brightness of His love.

He had found her . . . bone of His bone, flesh of His flesh. She was His desire,

> ⌒ *All wrongs had been made right. The maiden had been rescued from the dark nightmare and safely established in the kingdom of dreams.*

and she loved Him in a way she only dreamed possible. Never again would she be alone, for they were no longer two but one.

They traveled swiftly to his kingdom, where the bride was presented to his Father's house. Their union was blessed, and the bridal chamber awaited them. There their bodies danced to the song their souls had been singing. Now they were complete, and you know the ending . . . they lived happily ever after. All wrongs had been made right. The maiden had been rescued from the dark nightmare and safely established in the kingdom of dreams and light. The two had found each other. "Ever after" means from this moment forward, now and forever, never ceasing, for even the veil of death could not separate this love. For He is the Lord of life, and the dance always con-

> ⌒ *For He is the Lord of life, and the dance continues in another time and another place . . .*

tinues in another time and another place . . . where time has no end and there is joy unspeakable and beauty beyond description.

Is this your dream, your desire, your story? I believe it is, for Jesus is your Prince, and you long for His love deep within the recesses of your soul. It is a story so timeless and beautiful. It's been woven into the fiber of every woman's being. It is an attraction so strong and irresistible it causes the bride in each of us to cry out in unison with the Spirit, *Come Lord Jesus. Draw me, and I will run.*

Some of you may question this: *How could this possibly be my story, my dream, and my Prince? I didn't grow up in a palace. Often I pricked my finger and withdrew in pain, and no one woke me from my nightmare.* The reason you doubt the truth is you have spent too much time in the shadows of despair; you grew up and forgot the dreams of your childhood. It is time to awaken to His call and begin to dream again. I can say these things because I know He is there, waiting for you to turn His way. The end is not yet, and we have His sure and certain promise the day will come when each of us will encounter our faithful and loving Prince.

Therefore God exalted him to the highest place and gave him the name that is above every name, that at the name of Jesus every knee should bow, in heaven and on earth and under the earth, and every tongue confess that Jesus Christ is Lord, to the glory of God the Father. (Phil. 2:9–11)

He alone is the magnificent, faithful, and true Prince who left behind His heavenly kingdom to search for His captive bride. He is the Lover of our souls who still calls to us from the eons of ages, *Come away with me, My love!* He has broken the bonds of sin and banished the sleep of death from His beloved, and He bids her to dance, rejoice, and make herself ready for His return.

The only question that remains is, what will be our answer? Will we extend our hands toward Him and

> ⌒ *It is time to awaken to His call and begin to dream again.*

accept His embrace? Or will we turn our backs on all He has done to make us His own and slip back into an evil slumber of unbelief? On that day of His coming, will we be found on bended knee in a position of adoration, rejoicing in glorious wonder at the fulfillment of His promise, or will we be among those cowering in fear? I believe you are awakening to truth, and your face will be lifted in wonder. I believe you have this book in your hand because your heart yearns for your Prince.

There is another sleeping beauty found in the Bible. It is an area where we are encouraged to stay at rest, and to remain in a dreamlike state until the time of awakening, and that is the area of our sexual passion. It is to sleep and grow in longing and desire until the right moment. We are not the ones who determine when this wake-up call takes place. Humans are careless with timing, but God is not. We are charged to not awaken love until it desires (Song 2:7). Therefore our sexuality or sexual response to love could be likened to a *sleeping beauty*. Of course, this beauty does not rest under an evil spell, but dreams with anticipation of that moment. If He can be trusted to awaken us out of bondage, surely He can be trusted to awaken us to joy. To understand this further, let's turn to the wisdom found in the Song of Solomon.

> Daughters of Jerusalem, I charge you by the gazelles and by the does of the
> field: Do not arouse or awaken love until it so desires. (Song 2:7)

These are such passionate and poetic words I can almost picture the scene. In the distance, a herd of gazelles balances gracefully on legs of stilts as they graze the sunny slopes of distant foothills by a gently flowing stream. Under the cover of swaying branches, some timid does move slowly among the tender grass, occasionally lifting their graceful necks to study those who observe their tranquility. Their large, luminous eyes seem to look deep into your soul before their heads drop to pull up more fresh grass.

But what do these gently prancing gazelles and innocent, wide-eyed does of the field have to do with the arousal process of love? And since the charge is made to daughters of Jerusalem, are we even included in this? We have just discussed the beauty and hope of being awakened one day by a Prince, and here we are charged not to arouse or awaken natural love ourselves, but to wait. We are admonished concerning this not once, not twice, but three times in the Song of Solomon. In the New Living Translation, the instruction is a plea for a promise:

> Promise me, O women of Jerusalem, by the swift gazelles and the deer of the
> wild, not to awaken love until the time is right. (Song 3:5 NLT)

Here the timing of when love is to be awakened is more specifically outlined as "not . . . until the time is right." There is more energy in this admonishment than in others. You can almost picture the herd of gazelles swiftly traversing a field and effortlessly scaling the side of a hill that will take them from your sight. The deer in this verse are no longer as peaceful; they are restless and alert like wild deer breaking through the underbrush. Their heads lift and their antlers stand at attention, while their ears twitch to catch the slightest sound; at the mere snap of a twig, they will bolt and be gone. I don't know why, but I get the impression in this verse that our four-footed friends are running from something, not to it. The third warning is found in chapter 8:

I charge you, O daughters of Jerusalem, Do not stir up nor awaken love until it pleases. (Song 8:4 NKJV)

Notice again it is daughters, or women, who are charged to not awaken love from its sleep. It is not our place to awaken it, but the Prince's. I believe when we awaken love before the right time, it will be as fleeting in its beauty as the deer of the field, there one moment and gone from our sight the next. To possess the promise of sexual fulfillment without frightening it away requires patience.

My brethren, count it all joy when you fall into various trials, knowing that the testing of your faith produces patience. But let patience have its perfect work, that you may be perfect and complete, lacking nothing. (James 1:2–4 NKJV)

God wants this to be perfect for us. He wants the timing to be perfect. He wants us to be ready and perfectly positioned in a covenant when our love is awakened. He wants us to freely enjoy a garden of delight where there is no guilt or shame. Periods of anticipation create greater longing and desire in each lover, and the greater the desire, the stronger the passion and more ultimate the fulfillment. The most precious things of life often come at the expense of a waiting period. But they are ultimately worth it, for a longing fulfilled is a tree of life (Prov. 13:12). God's promise will always bring with it life.

To gain a greater understanding, let's examine the first time love was awakened between man and woman. We must return again to the Garden, where we find Adam desperately searching through the animals to find his counterpart. But of course, his soul mate was not found among the beasts or in the beauty of the Garden. Exhausted and lonely after a fruitless search, Adam was invited by God to rest.

> ∼ *Periods of anticipation create longing and desire, and the greater the desire, the stronger the passion and more ultimate the fulfillment.*

We are told God put Adam into a deep sleep, and while he rested,

Eve was brought forth. Adam dreamed, and his dream was given life. He'd never known love before, but he knew he would know her when he saw her. God comforted Adam, *Rest deeply, for you will never find what you look for in all your desperate searching. Sleep, dream, rest, and trust Me, and I will bring forth your deepest longing from your very side.*

Adam lay down and dreamed of what would be, what had to be, what he knew only in hope, for love always first begins with a dream. In order for dreams to move from the mist of night into the light of day, we must first surrender them to God. We realize our dreams when they are laid to rest on His altar. Death and disappointment are often the greatest pre-cursor to the fulfillment of our deepest desires.

Adam laid down his head, and with it, his search. Adam believed by lay-ing down his life, he would awaken to find his dream before him. Although love is always our desire and our dream, it must rest until the Prince of love arouses it. Why would He ever deny the ultimate fulfillment of the dreams He placed within us?

> You have granted him the desire of his heart and have not withheld the request of his lips. (Ps. 21:2)

It is time to rest and dream God's dream for you in the area of passion and sexuality. God is faithful to fulfill His promise and asks only that we trust His love and His dream for us. We must awaken from any hopeless, oppressive slumber and rest in His promises. We have His promise every-thing is under His control.

> "For I know the plans I have for you," declares the LORD, "plans to prosper you and not to harm you, plans to give you hope and a future."(Jer. 29:11)

He is our surety, for He cannot lie. Let's turn to Him now with these requests in prayer:

⌒ *Dear Heavenly Father,*

Thank You for sending Your Son to break through every bondage and to scale every wall, so that I might be awakened from my nightmares and transported to Your dream. I awake unto righteousness and embrace the light of truth. I will allow this area of passion to rest until You awaken it. I turn off every alarm clock that might awaken me too soon, and I quiet my soul with Your promises. I believe Your plans are not to harm me, but You delight in giving me a hope and a future. I believe You know me better than I even know myself, and so I place every unfulfilled dream at Your altar. I give You all my fears and disappointments. I will rest and dream safely in Your arms.

Love,
Your Daughter

6 The Original Cinderella

*H*ow does the Prince choose His bride? Is it by way of the ultimate beauty pageant? Assembled are the choicest daughters of earth. Each is perfect in beauty and form, talented and gifted, wealthy and educated, young and strong. As they come before Him, they are radiant and breathtaking. Each is persuasive as she makes her case as to why she should be His. The Prince listens attentively, agreeing they are indeed lovely. These women are elite and noble of breed . . . they are those we admire and wish to be more like. They're the "who's who" of this world's females. Yet even arrayed in all their beauty, they don't seem worthy of His majesty. None are.

Nevertheless, He has promised to choose one as His bride. When the last is finished, He calls for yet another, but there are no more. The Prince rises from His seat and parts the sea of loveliness to look at other daughters, those who remained in the shadows, the ones who didn't dare come before Him. He makes his way gently and tenderly through the disfigured, dysfunctional, demented, and uglier crowd, pressing deeper into the outer darkness until He has found just the one He is looking for. There is nothing beautiful about her . . . she is hideous, deformed, and on the verge of death. She has no nobility, a life conceived in sin, and utterly rejected even by her own. He towers over her cowering form and declares His bride!

Our Prince does not pursue the noble daughters of this world . . . it is not His way. He looks for the ones overlooked by others. He seeks them out because they are often hidden in the most wretched places, and discovered in deplorable conditions. It is His mission to find these rejected, bound, and abandoned ones, for He passionately loves the residents of hopeless and hideous situations.

I will search for the lost and bring back the strays. I will bind up the injured and strengthen the weak. (Ezek. 34:16)

Another Scripture states:

For the Son of Man came to seek and to save what was lost. (Luke 19:10)

Let's follow Him in His quest. It is a window into the life of a very different daughter than any you may know. Her birth was not planned or celebrated. Her arrival was not welcomed into the light or warmth of a home, but hurriedly concealed in cold, shadowy darkness. What becomes of these daughters? Those never hoped or prayed for, whose conceptions were wrought in a moment of groping passion, or even worse, violence, those formed in wombs of forbidden relationships, or monetary exchange. What of these?

Little ones born in secret then discarded. Abandoned without ever knowing the nurture and warmth of a mother's tender breast or the outline of a father's faces. Daughters whose fathers never thought twice about their fates and whose mothers never sang them a song, dried their tears, or touched them with tenderness. Instead, they're left alone naked and cold to die . . . without a backward glance or a second thought.

Let us look at one of these . . . an infant girl. Can you see her? She is cast aside in a field along a dusty road. Left to die unless someone would have pity on her. But who nurtures those rejected at birth? Does God turn His head away from the offspring of sin and resign them to a heritage of shame?

> ⌒ *Does God turn His head away from the offspring of sin and resign them to a heritage of shame?*

On the day you were born your cord was not cut, nor were you washed with water to make you clean, nor were you rubbed with salt or wrapped in cloths. No one looked on you with pity or had compassion enough to do any of these things for you. Rather, you were thrown out into the open field, for on the day you were born you were despised. (Ezek. 16:4–5)

The scene is repulsive and heartbreaking—a newborn girl thrashing about in a tangle of cord anchored to a withered placenta. What once sustained her life is cast upon her like a serpent. It stiffens in the hot sun, and with every movement entwines itself about her. The infant is covered with a residue of afterbirth and traces of her watery home. Her head is anointed with the birth blood of her mother, as her own ebbs away from the untied cord. It has mixed with the dust of the earth and turned it to rusty mud.

Let's lift our eyes from her . . . there is another character in this story. A Prince is out walking the fields. Perhaps it is a moment of meditation before His day begins. Let's shadow this noble and look through His eyes as He chances upon this abandoned daughter—or could it be He is actually looking for her? He hears a muffled cry and noise of her flailing rustles the golden stalks of wheat. He pauses and surveys His field. He hears it again . . . is it the whimper of a wounded animal? No, it is the plea of a fading infant. But he sees no workers. No mother in sight. He listens again; there it is, a whimper fading away as the bright sun climbs the morning sky. He turns aside, making His way cautiously through the field. The stalks murmur as He passes, making it difficult for Him to distinguish her movements. Then He sees her.

Then I passed by and saw you kicking about in your blood, and as you lay there in your blood I said to you, "Live!" (Ezek.16:6)

There she is kicking and flailing weakly in a muddy pool of blood and human filth. The scene is so hopeless, so helpless, he averts his eyes and wonders if it is too late for this little one. He is almost certain she is the daughter of a city prostitute who dwells in the shadows. An infant would have no value to such desperate women. He knows she is not the child of those who labor in his field . . . they would never throw one out like this. He pauses . . . is it better this way, for her to be born and die in secret? He looks again at the filthy, struggling infant. He sees something written across her forehead. It is a pronouncement of death, the parting word spoken by her mother: "Die!"

He bends closer and her eyes strain to focus on Him; something deep inside Him stirs. He lifts her from the filth and commands, "Live!" The cry rises from His very core, and with a single word, the King reverses the sen-

> ◠ He sees something written across her forehead. It is a pronouncement of death.

tence of death with the power of life. The infant shudders at the sound as she reaches toward His face. In the shadow of the Prince, she has found her reason to live.

His bloodstained hands quickly tie off her cord and stop the flow of blood. Then, in one motion, He removes His cloak and wraps her in the royal mantle of His house-

> ◠ In the shadow of the Prince, she has found her reason to live.

hold. He returns swiftly to His palace, where she is placed under the care of the very nurse who swaddled and nurtured Him. When asked who the child is and how long she'll stay, He answers without hesitation, "This little one is Mine . . . whose she was no longer matters. They forfeited all rights to her and left her to die without a name. I've redeemed her life. I am her benefactor and advocate."

She is bathed and rubbed with salt until all the filth of her shameful birth is removed. She is nursed and nurtured by the servants of the Prince's household, and when she is weaned and strong, the Prince places her in the home of the keeper of the fields and gardens. There she grows strong and eventually runs and plays in the field, never knowing her blood had spilled on its soil. She is told only that the Prince found her and made her His own. The Prince is a frequent visitor and always in the background, watching out for her and meeting her every need.

I made you grow like a plant of the field. You grew up and developed and became the most beautiful of jewels. Your breasts were formed and your hair grew, you who were naked and bare. (Ezek. 16:7)

In the beauty and provision of her surroundings, she flourishes like the produce of His royal fields, for the Prince has made her blossom. She lacks nothing, and her childhood is joyful. Looking at her, there is no trace of shame. She has *the noble appearance of one born of royalty. She is a stunning, vibrant jewel, reflecting and emitting the light of a love poured out so generously on her. Her breasts swell and form; hair grows, veiling her blossoming womanhood. There still is child in her and the time for love is not quite yet, but soon. Time passes.*

Later I passed by, and when I looked at you and saw that you were old enough for love, I spread the corner of my garment over you and covered your nakedness. I gave you my solemn oath and entered into a covenant with you, declares the Sovereign LORD, and you became mine. (Ezek. 16:8)

The Prince comes again, and when she runs to greet Him, He sees it is time. There is no child left in her. The transition is complete . . . she is a woman. Her breasts are full, her hips rounded, her legs long. She is old enough to give the love of a woman and to receive the love of a man. Yet she is uncovered. She is ready for a new covenant.

Again the Prince wraps His garment and arm around her and takes her for a walk. He pledges His life to her, not just as a benefactor but also as a husband. He spurns the princesses of royal birth to cherish forever this abandoned daughter found in a field. He knows she's loved Him as a brother, as a savior, and as a provider. He asks of her the love of a bride.

She can't believe her deepest dream is coming true. She is being offered the love of a Prince. She agrees with all her heart, and leaves behind the cottage to enter the royal household and begin the purification and beautification process. Handmaidens attend her every need as she makes herself ready for the Prince.

> ⌒ *He spurns the princesses of royal birth to cherish forever this abandoned daughter.*

I bathed you with water and washed the blood from you and put ointments on you. (Ezek. 16:9)

Her beautification start with a ritual cleansing of her menstrual blood, the sanctification of her sexuality, the separation of her fountain to the Lord of life. Fragrant ointments and oils are massaged into her freshly washed skin, moisturizing and perfuming as they ease away every place of dryness or irritation. She is like a wineskin being prepared for new wine.

She rests deeply now and dreams of her future with the Prince. He is the only man who ever loved her so deeply. The only One who ever spoke so tenderly to her. His love, provision, and goodness are all she's known. She relaxes and basks in the warmth of this.

The time comes to choose her wardrobe. Now, most brides must provide garments of their own, but hers are hand chosen and provided for by the Prince.

> I clothed you with an embroidered dress and put leather sandals on you. I dressed you in fine linen and covered you with costly garments. (Ezek. 16:10)

No expense is spared. Her garments are radiant, like the flowers of the Prince's garden. She is wrapped in the finest linen; over this are draped garments of such beauty they outshine the garments of the Prince. She has never known anything so beautiful. She runs her hand over each garment, almost unable to comprehend they are hers. Each garment is a declaration of His love and her royal position. With joy, she models them for the Prince as they share evening meals together. She is radiant. But there is more:

> ⌒ The Prince calls her altogether lovely.

> I adorned you with jewelry: I put bracelets on your arms and a necklace around your neck, and I put a ring on your nose, earrings on your ears and a beautiful crown on your head. (Ezek. 16:11–12)

Each day brings a new surprise. He encircles her svelte arms and wrists with bracelets. Her regal neck is anchored with a beautiful necklace. He frames her face with ear and nose rings, and then places a magnificent crown upon her head. The Prince calls her altogether lovely. No one would ever guess the origin of her shadowy birth. She is the radiant reflection of His tender care and passionate love.

> So you were adorned with gold and silver; your clothes were of fine linen and costly fabric and embroidered cloth. (Ezek. 16:13a)

She is accessorized with the gold of sunlight and the silver of moonlight. They sparkle and dance against her skin. Her linen undergarments are overlaid with the finest silks and woven fabrics. Each is uniquely crafted for her alone. The Prince has ordered it to be so. None can match her beauty.

Your food was fine flour, honey and olive oil. You became very beautiful and rose to be a queen. (Ezek. 16:13b)

He feeds her the finest grains, the sweetest honey, and the richest oil. She feasts on His goodness, and her beauty elevates her. The night of the wedding feast is appointed; the guests are invited, for the time has come for their love to be celebrated. Everyone has been whispering and wondering about the identity of the Prince's bride. Where was she from . . . what did she look like? Many have questioned the Prince's wisdom—why not take a bride of royal birth and stature? Why this one? Then they see her and know. She is the perfect reflection of His love. She is seated at His right hand with His banner above her head. When she rises from the feast, she is swept up into His arms and carried into His royal bedchamber. There she becomes His princess. Their love is beautiful, tender, and passionate. He loves her in the secret place, and it soon becomes evident to all, for no one can be loved by a Prince and keep it a secret.

> ⌒ No one can be loved by a Prince and keep it a secret.

And your fame spread among the nations on account of your beauty, because the splendor I had given you made your beauty perfect, declares the Sovereign LORD. (Ezek. 16:14)

The longing of every woman . . . to be perfect and perfectly loved. It was not something she could ever have achieved alone. Yes, she was beautiful, but the Prince magnified her beauty by adding something only a Prince can . . . *splendor.* Splendor is otherworldly; it is a glimpse of heaven while here on earth. The word *splendor* encompasses a magnificence transcending earthly comprehension. It takes our breath away with its brilliance, majesty, and grandeur. Was this the beauty that veiled Eve in the Garden of God's creation? Was it the radiance, the brilliance that slipped away and left her feeling naked, ashamed, and in need of a covering? Perhaps.

This is a Cinderella story of a much deeper magnitude. There are no dead parents, just those who didn't care

> ∽ *This is a Cinderella story of a much deeper magnitude.*

enough to stay; no evil stepmother tolerates this daughter of ashes, for she was not left by the warmth of a fire. There is no fairy godmother to give her beauty enough to attract a Prince. She is discovered nameless and in her most helpless state, and she is loved before there is ever a reason. There is no midnight deadline but a never-ending covenant. And instead of a fragile glass slipper, there is splendor . . . garments of light to cast aside any question of whom she belongs to.

Though most of us were not left to die in an open field at birth, on some level each of us identifies with this dream. It must be so, for God placed His dream in the heart of every woman. This story is so much more than the rescue of an abandoned, rejected daughter. It is even greater than its prophetic application for Israel and the Church. It speaks to us even now, commanding us to *live* with the Prince and not die in our sin. He sets before us life and death, blessing and cursing, and He shouts, "Choose life!" With an offer of love so gracious, how could there be any question? Surely this abandoned daughter understands the depth of His mercy and grace. Surely she and the princely King will live happily ever after. I hate the ending of this story. For it is more heartbreaking than her birth.

> But you trusted in your beauty and used your fame to become a prostitute. You lavished your favors on anyone who passed by and your beauty became his. (Ezek. 16:15)

Something has gone terribly wrong! How could one who was loved so completely and cared for so tenderly turn away from a love so great, so noble, and so pure? Why would she trust in the beauty cultivated by the Prince when she could trust in Him? Why would she use honor and fame to attract men and demote herself from a princess to a prostitute? Why lavish favors on those who gave nothing to her, on those who passed her by when she was dying, ugly, and naked?

If we're honest, most of us can search our hearts, examine our actions, and find ourselves guilty of unfaithfulness to our Prince. Perhaps we've not trusted in our beauty or fame, but slowly turned from our first and faithful love to seek out affirmation from this faithless world.

Our Prince is always willing to cleanse and beautify rejected and abandoned women. He rescued each of us from sin and reversed our sentence of death. He severed our connections with our past and dealt mercifully with our issues . . . issues of promiscuity, issues of abortion, issues of insecurity, issues of blood. Will we allow His love to be enough? Or look elsewhere for fulfillment? Will the blessing of His favor turn our heads, and with it our hearts, from the very One who sanctified and made us perfect with His splendor? What will our responses be to His goodness and mercy? Will we put aside the garments of rejection and allow the spirit of adoption to have its way, or will we look for our fulfillment in multiple sexual affirmations of our attractiveness?

> ⌒ *Our Prince is always willing to cleanse and beautify rejected and abandoned women.*

How many arms must we feel around us before we finally say, "It is enough . . . I am whole"?

If we trust in our beauty, we'll constantly need to look to others to reaffirm our value and desirability. Our self-worth will be jeopardized and threatened by other women around us.

Look again at the provisions for this abandoned daughter: They are lavish, extravagant, and far beyond generous. We'd consider her a fool for spurning so great a love, and label her unworthy . . . but before we go there with her, let's see the lesson for each of us in her story.

This is a story of redemption, and in it, none are found worthy. It is the longing of a Prince for a bride on whom to lavish His love and provision. One who's thankful for His goodness and responds with passionate love . . . a bride who has glimpsed His radiant face and no longer desires the face of another.

It is the story of us. We were without hope and dying, even as our very life began. But the Prince heard you cry out from your field of pain, suffering, and sin. He saw you when you were helpless and hopeless in the filth of rejection and blood of sin. He was moved with compassion and reversed the curse of death, then cleansed you from the sin and filth of your past. He provided for and tenderly nurtured each of us, and we blossomed in His love, but sometimes He seems so faraway and distant, a dream waiting to come.

It is then we're tempted to turn to others. We wanted to be touched here and now rather than wait. We take off garments of splendor and put on gaudy ones in order to gather the trinkets of these liaisons and forget the promise of glorious jewels. Too often the deceitfulness of present riches and the lust of other things distort the promises of the Prince. So some of us have undressed in the presence of men with whom we had no covenant, hoping their bodies would make us whole, but their hands only dirtied again the very places the Prince had so carefully cleansed.

But I believe better of you. This book is in your hands, for His name is written upon your heart.

⌒ Dear Heavenly Father,

I am overwhelmed by the beauty of Your mercy and the depths of Your love. You searched me out when I was dying in my sin and brought me into Your household. You have clothed my nakedness and cleansed me of every issue of blood and sin in my life. Thank You for Your forgiveness, mercy, and tender care. Forgive me for taking the beauty You have given me and looking for affirmation from the sons of earth when I already have a covenant of splendor. I renounce my other lovers and pursue You alone. Thank You for loving me in my frailty and not merely in my beauty. I am the Cinderella whom You have drawn from the ashes. I set my heart on You, for You are my one true Prince.

Love,
Your Daughter

7 What to Do If Sexual Love Awakens

We have spoken of the virtues of allowing our romantic and sexual responses to rest and remain in a dreamlike state until they are awakened by the kiss of the Prince, but what if they have already been aroused by another and are raring to go? What if sexual desire refuses to be lulled back to sleep without a fight? If this is your state, you are already aware how much more difficult it is to return desire back to a state of sleep after it has been awakened, especially if its awakening was sudden, rude, or premature. This leaves us with our adrenaline rushing in its wake of excitement or fright.

Add to this the fact that it is difficult to float back to sleep when everywhere you look there are enticements and alarms sounding telling you to stay awake or you'll miss something! To restore a dreamlike bliss, the atmosphere surrounding us must contain some kind of buffer to maintain peace and quiet. Awakened desires must be handled carefully to reconstruct a setting for peaceful dreams, for once fears or desires have been aroused, they are hard to quiet. And there is a reason for this: Our desires were never meant to be awakened and then neglected. This is true of any human appetite.

> ⌒ *Our desires were never meant to be awakened and then neglected.*

I remember when my boys were infants; I nursed them exclusively for the first six months before introducing food into their diets . . . and with their first tastes of food, everything changed. Before these first encounters, they would sit contentedly in my lap at restaurants and never pay much attention to the food that moved freely past them across the tables. They simply smiled at the waiters and other patrons in happy oblivion. They were aware of different and delicious smells, but they were uninterested because they had no idea what they were missing. Until, of course, they tasted food for themselves, and then it was a whole other story!

Now the smell of food drove them wild. When their appetites were awakened, they no longer smiled passively at the people who passed (unless as a sort of bribe). Their focus was on acquiring food! If I held them in my lap as I ate, they were after my fork or spoon regardless of what was on it, or they pulled at the tablecloth in an attempt to transfer the food into my lap and within their reach. Strapping them into a high chair isolated them but didn't stop their missions unless food was on their tray. They were single-minded in purpose. They'd tasted and found the food to be good. They'd developed a taste for food and were not happy until they had it!

Therefore, I was always careful never to introduce food and awaken this appetite until they were first physically ready to consume it, and second, I was prepared to provide it on a regular basis. This had nothing to do with the desirability of food . . . I am certain before the age of six months they would have enjoyed the taste of food, but their sensitive digestive systems would not have been mature enough to handle it. Food is, of course, both good and necessary to our nourishment, growth, and development, but if food is given too soon, allergies or intolerances may develop. If food is allowed a wrong position of prominence in our lives, the appetite or desire for it may control or drive us to abuse it even though it is good and delicious. We may develop an unhealthy appetite for certain types of food that tantalize our taste buds but are void of any real nutritional value.

Indulging this type of appetite eventually leads to the abuse of food. Abuse is the wrong use of something. Therefore, *food* is not what is bad in the equation, but the *misuse* of it is. When we abuse or misuse what is good, it becomes destructive and empowered in

> ⌒ *When we abuse or misuse what is good, it becomes destructive.*

> ⌒ *Our sexual appetite is not unlike our appetite for food . . . it too remains dormant until it is awakened by outside stimuli.*

our lives. In this case, our desire or appetite is no longer our servant, but it becomes a master that demands satisfaction.

Our sexual appetite is not unlike our appetite for food . . . it too remains dormant until it is awakened by outside stimuli. Just as we cannot live without food, we cannot reproduce or give life without sexual union. This makes the appetite for both necessary and vital to the propagation of life. But just as our appetites for food can drive us, so can our aroused sexual desires if we do not manage and master them. In this chapter, we are going to address both spiritual and practical ways of facing off with raging sexual appetites.

Let's go back to the parallel of food so we can move from the everyday towards the more sensitive issues. We will begin with the development of a taste or the whetting of an appetite for something. I will use myself as an example here. I wonder if I would still occasionally crave good dark chocolate if I had never tasted it. And what about coffee? If I'd never stirred a heaping tablespoon of Breyer's coffee ice cream into my cup of java, and sprinkled cinnamon on top, in a desperate attempt to stay awake one morning, would I still being drinking mocha lattes twelve years later?

Of course I wouldn't! And I wouldn't even know what I was missing. I wouldn't have developed a taste for these delicious things. As long as I only knew coffee as a thick, black, bitter liquid, I despised it. As long as chocolate was only in the form of white or milk, I had no trouble resisting it.

Actually there is no struggle! I do not fight my occasional urge for chocolate or my morning ritual of flavored coffee . . . I indulge them! They are not my masters, but a sort of comfort ritual I go through. I can go a week or more without dark chocolate, and no one will be hurt. I will not be grumpy, but I do enjoy it when I have it. As far as the coffee, if I want to wake up suddenly instead of slowly emerging from a fog, I drink it.

Perhaps I am not being fair to use these as examples. These are yummy though not necessarily nutritious treats, but please indulge me. What if I allowed my enjoyment of them to override my desire for other healthy foods? What if I decided the sensual pleasure (provided by the dark chocolate) and the heightened state of awareness (supplied by the coffee) were more important than any other feelings in my life? Perhaps then mixed green salads would no longer have any appeal, because they didn't make me feel the same way chocolate did. After all, a salad would be crunchy and cold, while in contrast, dark chocolate is silky and warm. Maybe water would just not do it for me, because it just didn't have the kick coffee gave or provide the warmth and rush I was looking for.

I would slowly but surely find all cuisine that did not share their tastes and textures or arouse the same feelings boring and mundane. What if I slipped away from reality and for two weeks existed solely on the merits of chocolate and coffee? I'd be happy, thin, and awake . . . at least for a while. Then everything would tilt out of balance, and my appetites would have to be brought back into check.

My point is, we develop our own appetites and desires. We can increase or diminish their influences by the importance we assign them. We can

> ⟿ *We develop our own appetites and desires.*

control their influences by limiting our intake. Here's a case in point.

When I was working on my first book, *Out of Control and Loving It*, I had just had my fourth son, Arden, and coffee had become way too good of a friend. With two preschool children at home, I discovered the best time to write was between the hours of 10 P.M. and 2 A.M. I would wake up to a large mug and a half of coffee, and then as I began to fade in the afternoon, I'd have another round (my version of English tea). This supplied me with enough energy to keep going until two and sometimes even three in the morning. I'd tumble into bed, then wake at 6:30 A.M. and start the whole routine again. I remember the most difficult part was getting the coffee made, but after a few sips, everything was easier. This went on for weeks, then the weeks gave way to months. My face didn't even seem to look the same if java was not coursing through my veins.

Then one night it all changed. I had stayed on my regular schedule and had just completed my 10 P.M. nursing of Arden and successfully laid him down for the night. (In contrast to the times when he remained attached while I typed.) With a sigh and a prayer, I sat down to type. The words were coming fast and furious, and then suddenly around 2 A.M. I realized my body was listing drastically to one side. I straightened up and returned to my typing only to sense my body falling away to the left again. I thought, *What is going on here?* I stood up to stretch and found the room spinning, even though my mind was still clicking away and totally coherent. I reasoned perhaps I was more tired than I knew, and I closed up shop and headed downstairs to bed. I found myself having trouble negotiating the stairs, and then I walked right into the doorframe of my bedroom even though I had intended fair clearance. I tumbled into bed and felt as though my body was spinning even as my mind raced on various tangents. I thought, *Something is not right.* Obviously, my body was exhausted, but my mind was still going. I lay there for hours, unable to sleep or to quiet my mind. I was tired, but as soon as I drifted to sleep, my mind would race and jerk me awake. As the morning light drifted through my window, I was certain it must be the coffee.

Never one to be accused of being balanced, I cut myself off cold turkey. I was foggy all day and more than a little edgy. My little ones were begging me to embrace the cup, but I refused. Sometime in the early evening, a headache of proportions I'd previously believed impossible began. I am not one given to headaches, and before this secretly thought they were attention-getting devices for hypochondriacs. Now I was the one rummaging through my cabinets in a desperate attempt to find a Tylenol sample I'd thrown in for a rainy day. It only barely took the edge off the vise now attached to my head. I never wanted to go through withdrawals from caffeine again, so I avoided coffee for the next three years. Then one cold, Colorado morning, I sipped the cup again and was able to properly reintroduce it into my life without substituting it on a daily basis for sleep.

Now, I am going to push the envelope a little further and tie together the concepts of sex and coffee and chocolate, for illustrative purposes. Like coffee, sex makes us feel vibrantly alive and awake, actually more so than anything else in our lives. And sex is delicious like chocolate.

Sex creates a high that nothing else can reach. It is the convergence of so many sensations at once with endorphins going wild. It is both a sensation overload and a fleeting glimpse of heaven.

> ⌒ *When awakened at the wrong time, desire becomes lust, and lust is restless.*

This makes it hard to do without once we have sampled its wine.

In light of all this, it is understandable that we would initially want to satiate our desire rather than put it to rest, especially when it brings us so much pleasure and makes us feel so alive, desirable, and temporarily whole. But there is another element we need to examine as well: when it is not the right time for love, sexual desire is always the wrong thing, no matter how pleasurable the sensations. When awakened at the wrong time, desire becomes lust, and lust is restless and shrouded in shame.

Love needs to rest so it can awaken again later, not in the form of lust, but in a truer and more beautiful state. This additional rest allows it to awaken at the appropriate hour, renewed and more powerful in pleasure and passion. Then we will not be disappointed, abandoned, or under torment. We want to put lust to death, and in its place resurrect love without a trace of guilt or shame to rob from her beauty. How can all this be accomplished?

The process is not unlike how a restless or frightened child is lulled back to sleep. When my children are frightened, injured, ill, or overly excited, I draw them close to quiet them. To do this, I may rock them, or lie down next to them in their beds, or if the hour is late, I may bring them into my own bed. Regardless of the method, I want them to know I am near. Once they are comfortable and in my arms, I listen to their fears. The story of an injury or the terror of a nightmare is shared while I stroke their hair or trace their features. When they are spent of their burdens or I can sense the further telling of them will no longer help, I begin speaking back to them in a whisper of a voice to quiet their excited tones.

In these whispers I reaffirm God's love and mine and remind them of His faithful protection. Then I speak truths of greater power and paint images of greater beauty than the frightening shadows of lies and fear. I

> *When we hurt, when we fail, when we are frightened, God wants us to draw near, never away.*

sing lullabies until I can tell by their breathing they are deep in sleep.

These aspects of a mother's tender response to her frightened children are drawn from the heart of God. They are but a small reflection of His desire to comfort our storms and chase away our fears. When we hurt, when we fail, when we are frightened, God wants us to draw near, never away. As His children, we are invited to draw near into His arms of safety and love. There He will give us visions of beauty capable of putting us again at ease and rest.

I love the safety of this image of a Father tenderly rocking His daughter back to sleep so she can rest and heal. I know you may be frightened that if you allow desire to return to sleep it may never be awakened or fulfilled again. These are haunting questions: If I let this area of my life go, will I ever see it again? Will God really meet these needs in my life? If I yield to God now, will He be faithful to fulfill me by His promise of a future hope?

I believe with all my heart that your Father God wants to do the following for you by His Spirit and through this book:

- draw you near

- wash every trace of guilt and shame from you

- lay aside your fears by addressing them in the light of truth

- give you a hope and a future

- rock you until your storm is calmed

- return you to rest

- restore the dream in your heart

Once after I spoke on some of these issues, a beautiful young girl came up to me for prayer. She confessed that she had compromised areas of purity to gain the affection and attention of boys, and she didn't know how to recover herself and return to her dream. I held her in my arms and prayed with her, and while I was praying, I heard God whisper a promise for her. He promised that as she pressed into Him with songs of worship and praise, He would in turn sing over her a lullaby to put to rest what had been awakened deep within her.

> ⌒ He promised that as she pressed into Him with songs of worship and praise, He would in turn sing over her a lullaby to put to rest what had been awakened.

I was overwhelmed by the love in His tone. There was no shame or condemnation in His words, only a promise to sing away her fears, guilt, and shame. As she drew near, He promised to draw her to Himself and hide her safely in the shadow of His wing. This Scripture gives us a beautiful image of His tenderness:

> The LORD your God is with you, he is mighty to save. He will take great delight in you, he will quiet you with his love, he will rejoice over you with singing. (Zeph. 3:17)

This image speaks multitudes. He isn't aloof and unapproachable, but quickly comes to our aid and with His great might saves us. He doesn't reject or condemn us when we cry out in fear or helplessness. He delights in quieting His children just as any mother considers it a joy to comfort her own. But there are limits to a mother's comfort . . . my might only goes so far, but His is limitless, like His love. The depth of it quiets us, and then He sings to us. It is such a compelling image that it invites each of us to draw near and let Him quiet the storms we cannot. In this place we are allowed to rest, and soon we find ourselves joining Him in song.

> I will praise you as long as I live, and in your name I will lift up my hands. My soul will be satisfied as with the richest of foods; with singing lips my mouth will praise you. On my bed I remember you; I think of you through

the watches of the night. Because you are my help, I sing in the shadow of your wings. My soul clings to you; your right hand upholds me. (Ps. 63:4–8)

I cannot overemphasize the importance of praising Him. There is amazing power in music, and never before has there been such a rich array of powerful praise and worship songs available to us. As we already discussed, music is the language of the heart, for it has the power to bypass our heads. When we praise Him, we feast on His faithfulness. He prepares a banquet of the richest array of costly foods to strengthen us. If on our beds we remember Him, He will remain with us through the watches of the night.

Often when I lie down with one of my children, he will repeatedly wake himself until he is certain of my presence. Now I must admit, I do wait until he is deep in sleep, then I slip away from his bunk bed to the comfort of my own. But not God; He stays. He tucks us under the shadow of His wings while we sing. Praising Him causes our souls to cling to Him, and then His right hand upholds us. The joy of the Lord becomes our strength, and His strength is something you will need when you are battling an appetite.

Like Esther, we need to set aside a time to fast from our desires as we prepare a banquet for His delight. We bring before Him the feast of our wills and exchange our delights and desires for His. Our praise and worship is a banquet that honors Him, and there He prepares a table before us in the presence of our enemies. Like Esther, I am crying out for the daughters of this generation that they might be spared the destruction of the enemy of their souls, who seeks to sell them to death. You can do the same. It is our time as women to lay down our lives to preserve the lives of many daughters yet unknown to us.

> ⌒ There is only one way to dismantle a desire, craving, or appetite . . . you have to starve.

There is only one surefire way to dismantle a desire, craving, or appetite . . . you have to starve it to death. You must destroy it and render it powerless by cutting off its food supply. Do you know the saying, *an army marches on its stomach?* Well, you are about to cut off the food supply to the enemy camp. You are going to have to face off with your soul and tell it who is boss.

In Psalm 35:13, King David shared how he humbled himself with fasting. When our bodies and souls rage out of control, we need to take it down a few notches by reminding it that God is in charge. It is only flesh, and we will not be dominated by its appetites.

Whenever I have needed a major breakthrough, especially in wrestling matches with my flesh, I have always turned to fasting. In fact, I can't even imagine attempting spiritual warfare without fasting on some level because it is such a powerful and effective weapon. Even Jesus, the Son of God, fasted. I am afraid that today most Christians are quicker to embrace a diet than a fast. They hope to change their outward appearances while remaining inwardly bound, but that's a whole other story. Here I want to share with you truths with the power to set you free:

> Is not this the kind of fasting I have chosen: to loose the chains of injustice and untie the cords of the yoke, to set the oppressed free and break every yoke? (Isa. 58:6)

God's chosen fast accomplishes the following: it breaks the chains of injustice, unties the cords that hold the yoke in place, frees the oppressed, and then breaks *every* yoke—not just the easy ones, but every one. No yoke is safe from the power of a fast. Is sexual sin a yoke? Definitely! Yokes direct and restrict the movements and actions of their bearers. They take them in captivity to places they do not wish to go. Yokes exhaust us under their weight. But as we put on our garments of praise for this spirit of heaviness, we will begin to feel some relief as God gives us His strength so we can face off with it and break free!

In my example of the coffee abuse, I am sure you remember that I took the drastic approach and stopped my coffee consumption cold turkey. If you are indulging a sexual appetite, I would suggest the drastic and immediate cut off course for you as well.

Put a knife to your throat if you are a man given to appetite. (Prov. 23:2 NKJV)

That sounds pretty serious to me. Here are some more Scriptures:

Flee from sexual immorality. All other sins a man commits are outside his body, but he who sins sexually sins against his own body. (1 Cor. 6:18)

Flee the evil desires of youth, and pursue righteousness, faith, love and peace, along with those who call on the Lord out of a pure heart. (2 Tim. 2:22)

The word *flee* is strong and urgent. The first time we find it used is when the angels tell Lot to get out of town (Gen. 19:17). It means to run from something in terror. There is nothing casual about this admonishment. In order to flee, you are going to have to fast!

You definitely don't want to end up like Lot, fleeing a town of immorality under the judgment of God, only to end up drunk in a cave having sex with his daughters. When you flee, you must run without looking back. Go to the shelter of God, not to the shelter of drunkenness or some other form of bondage. When you flee, you drop the baggage!

Let us lay aside every weight, and the sin which so easily ensnares us, and let us run with endurance the race that is set before us. (Heb. 12:1 NKJV)

Fasting is the ultimate in life's weight reduction. It is a stripping away from the body and soul of the things that hold us down and tether us to this earth. When we fast, our loads are lightened, and our spirits are set free! Fasting is the ultimate example and expression of submission to God, and when we submit to God we are no longer running in terror; we are running with purpose, and the enemy flees!

Submit yourselves, then, to God. Resist the devil, and he will flee from you. (James 4:7)

When we humble ourselves and hide in the shadow of His wing, the enemy looks for us and sees only Him, for we are hidden. In the shelter of His wing, there is no lack of authority or power. As we stop feeding other areas of our lives, we become hungry and thirsty for more of Him. He transforms our appetites and feeds us on His goodness and loving-kindness, which is so much better for us than earthly delights. (Even coffee and chocolate!)

Here are my suggestions for your fast. First, remember that this is not a time of denial for you, but for your flesh. Remember that your spirit is willing . . . it is your flesh we're going to make uncomfortable. Therefore spiritually, this is a time of celebration, of feasting and joy! Remember while Esther fasted, she prepared a lavish banquet for the king. You are going to indulge the King, not your flesh. When you honor the King, He will honor you with His presence. Approach this as a privilege, not a punishment.

> ⁓ *You are going to indulge the King, not your flesh.*

Next, realize this as a life-and-death issue, because it is. You are putting bondage to death.

For if you live according to the sinful nature, you will die; but if by the Spirit you put to death the misdeeds of the body, you will live. (Rom. 8:13)

Since something is going to have to die in the process, let it be the sinful nature and the misdeeds of the body. Again, like Esther, take it seriously. If at all possible, begin with a three-day food fast. Even if you work, you can start it on Thursday at sundown and end it Sunday at sundown. I would suggest a juice or water fast for these days. You can find resource materials on this at any health-food store. *This book is not intended to provide medical advice or to take the place of medical advice and treatment from your personal physician, so I advise you to consult your own doctor or other qualified health professionals regarding fasting if you have any concerns about it. If you are under age eighteen, do not fast without discussing it with your parents first.* I personally drink nonacidic juices and distilled water during my fasts.

There is no sense in denying yourself food if you don't indulge yourself in God. Gather everything you need beforehand so you can just rest during your fast. Unplug your phone, turn off your TV, and put away the magazines. Crank the stereo with praise and worship music only. Stay away from secular love songs and just spend this time alone, being intimate with Him. This is a Sabbath time, so don't work on other things. Rest, sleep and draw close to Him. Read the Word, including the book of Esther and the promises for fasting, or other Christian works that challenge you.

> ⌒ *There is no sense in denying yourself food if you don't indulge yourself in God.*

During the fast, you are not just starving your flesh; you are strengthening your spirit. Keep a journal of your prayer requests for this time. Make these petitions known as you go through this time. Pour out your heart like water before the Lord. Tell Him every fear and hope, be open and honest with Him. Record what He shows you through Scripture and prayer.

Come boldly before Him. Like Esther, put on your royal robes (of righteousness in Christ) and stand in the inner court of the palace, in front of the king's hall (Est. 5:1). Know that He will be pleased to see you, and He will extend His royal scepter of favor in your direction. When He asks what you want, tell Him you have come to invite Him to a banquet of worship and adoration, and when you have feasted together, make your petitions known.

During this time, go through your house and rid it of everything unclean or displeasing to the Lord. The Holy Spirit will show you these items, so be sensitive and obedient to His leading. This *may* mean inappropriate videos, books, letters, music, or even pictures of old boyfriends. Anything that encourages impurity should definitely be suspect. As you offer up your sexuality as an offering of fragrant worship before the Lord, ask Him if there are any other areas He would desire, and offer those before Him as well. Make this a time to love Him with your whole being, and He will give you living water and nourishment you previously could not have imagined.

I want to pray with you as you set off on this great adventure.

> ⌒ *Dear Heavenly Father,*
>
> *I set my heart in agreement with my sister as she comes before You. Draw her near, and wash away every trace of guilt and shame as You push away her fears, causing them to flee in the light of Your truth. Renew her hope and give her a future. Hold her close in Your arms and rock her until every storm is calmed. Give her rest, and restore to her Your dream for her life. Hide her in the shadow of Your wing, and put a song in her heart. Sing over her and quiet her with Your love. Replace any garment of shame with the beautiful and glorious robe of righteousness. Plant for her a garden of delight, and let this be the beginning of special and intimate times of fellowship. As she rests in You, do war on her behalf. We love You, Father, and thank You that You have set us free! Destroy every yoke, and loose every area of bondage. Raise us up to be shining beacons to this generation.*
>
> *Love,*
> *Your Daughter*

Feel free to add your own words to mine, but know that this prayer has already been prayed with you . . . our hearts have already joined together in this song.

8 Honoring Your Father

I recently received a call from a desperate mother. Her daughter had confessed she was sexually involved with a dangerous young man. The mother was horrified and wanted very much to protect her daughter. In the past they'd unknowingly put her in harm's way. She'd lost her virginity. Now it was happening again. The mother hoped I'd meet with them and pray for her daughter so further tragedy could be averted.

But I was rather doubtful. I learned long ago when people know right from wrong and still choose wrong, you can talk and pray with them until you are blue in the face but nothing changes until there is a change of heart. So I questioned further.

> *When people know right from wrong and still choose wrong . . . nothing changes until there is a change of heart.*

"This guy is not a Christian, and your daughter knew her involvement was wrong. She needs to get away from him. I'm sure you've told her this. Why would talking to me make any difference? If *she* really wants this meeting, I will come, but if not, it will be just a waste of everyone's time."

The mother sounded desperate and broken. She assured me her daughter was sincere and explained she'd even stayed home from school in the hope of our meeting. I agreed to meet later that day.

I scampered about to squeeze into my already full morning a meeting I hadn't planned for. I showered and was out the door as quickly as I could. On the way to the meeting, I prayed for God's wisdom, guidance, and anointing to be present. The mother and daughter were waiting for me at the restaurant. I sat and the daughter shared how she had met this boy two weeks earlier at a gas station and knew he was trouble right away. She heard a voice say, *Stay away from him*, but she didn't. He'd already managed to seduce her and gain access to her bank account. He'd been kicked out of school, and even his father had warned her to stay away from him. But she didn't listen. She wanted to rehabilitate and help him in some way. Now she was scared he might be in some legal trouble, and she might be implicated. The stress became overwhelming, and she told her mother the whole story. She was afraid she couldn't get away from him because he kept calling her on her cell phone.

I cut to the chase. "You know, this guy sounds like he would make an excellent pimp. Do you know most prostitutes are trying to save their pimps and help them out? You are seventeen, and he is twenty-something. No offense, but he doesn't want your help the way you want to give it. You need to let God heal you first and find out why you have such bad taste in men."

Mother and daughter nodded their agreement, so I continued.

"You need to close your bank account. Change your cell number, and tell him you won't be seeing him anymore."

The girl looked doubtful, "I don't know . . . when I'm with him I have a hard time saying no."

"You aren't going to be with him. You are going to flee fornication. If you can't do it over the phone, then ask your father to help you out. I am sure he will have no problem telling this young man he can't see you again. Perhaps he could meet him at the door with a shotgun when he makes the announcement. Let your father protect you. That's what daddies are for."

Mother and daughter exchanged glances, and it was then I realized the father was totally unaware of what was going on.

"Your husband doesn't know yet?" I asked the mother.

She explained she had just found out herself, and although the father knew about the first young man, he didn't know about this one. He didn't like this young man from the start, and they knew he'd be disappointed and heartbroken if he learned of this situation.

I asked the girl to promise to do three things for me. First, to tell her father the whole ugly truth, next to ask him to act as her protector with this guy, and then to buy and read a particular book and her Bible each day while God walked her through this process. I gave her a loose gemstone. I told her how this ugly, frightening place of hardship could become a jewel in her life if she would learn from it. Then we went out to my car and prayed.

But I didn't sense any relief. It was as though I was to magically break something off her that deep down inside she wanted to keep but was afraid one day she might not be able to handle. I left frustrated, even though she had assured me she would do all we discussed.

I never heard from them again, but they did go to a friend of mine the following week. It seemed the mother was desperate again; the daughter had gone out with this young man Saturday after we'd met and failed to come home at all.

Are you as confused as I am? I have only sons. If my boys came home with this kind of story about some girl, do you think I'd allow them out with her on Saturday? I believe as long as they live in your home, you are obligated to protect them, especially if they're minors. I'm not sure where the ball was dropped with this young girl. I don't know if she snuck out without her parents' knowledge or if the father was never told. Or whether guilt manipulated the situation, and they felt powerless because they'd failed her in the past, so they could no longer protect her in the future.

> ⁓ *Parents, protect your children. Women, take back your power, and walk in godliness.*

But it is not too late. We must cry out. Parents, protect your children. Women, take back your power, and walk in godliness. This begins by applying the wisdom and counsel of God. We must humble ourselves and acknowledge His ways are truly higher than ours. After all, our thoughts and wisdom are mere foolishness in the light of His counsel.

A generation of fathers needs to be heartbroken and outraged at the merchandising, molestation, and rape of their daughters. They need to repent of being weak, and then rise up, protect them, and bring healing to the places they've left vulnerable. Women should be protected rather than violated by the men in their lives.

Fathers must be the protectors of virtue for their daughters. Girls who enjoy a healthy, vibrant relationship with their fathers are much less vulnerable to abusive men. Because they have enjoyed healthy role models in their homes they recognize an unhealthy relationship when they see it.

> ⌒ *A generation of fathers needs to be heartbroken and outraged at the merchandising, molestation, and rape of their daughters.*

Daughters treated as royal daughters of the King are less likely to allow anyone else to treat them in a lesser manner. Fathers who compliment and affirm their daughters protect them from looking for other men to do this for them. Fathers who remember what they or their friends were like when they were teenagers are much less likely to allow their daughters to be put into positions where they can be compromised. Fathers who openly train and instruct their daughters in the matters of male and female relationships are equipping their daughters with the knowledge they need to make good decisions in tempting situations. Conversely, girls with angry fathers who seem never to be pleased with them will look for male affirmation somewhere else.

I remember when I went away to college, everything changed. I had traveled far from my midwestern home in frigid Indiana to sunny Arizona. I was very excited about being totally free from all parental control and peer expectations. I could leave my awkwardness behind and make a new start. I went through sorority rush and pledged a house before the first semester of school began. This gave me an automatic group of friends to start the year off with. I was enjoying a lot of attention from boys, and this was quite a contrast to my high-school days when I was virtually ignored. When I walked into my classes or around the campus, I was flirted with, whistled at, or asked out. All the attention made my head spin, because I had known mostly name calling and jeers during the previous four years.

I pretended to handle it well, but inside I was shaky and unsure of myself. I began to find strength by drawing male attention, even though at one level it frightened me. I was afraid if they got too close they would find I was really a loser posing to be cool. Because of this, I toyed with most of the boys I dated. If they started to like me too much, I dumped them. I would brag I believed in changing men like I changed my underwear . . . a new one for each new day. In one semester, I dated forty-five guys! This only shows just how terrified I was of intimacy.

But at the close of the year, I met my match. I was eighteen, and he was twenty-seven. He was tall, handsome, and worldly, and I found out later he was a sexual predator. He stalked freshman girls, and he had set his sights on me. He wasn't even a student, just a guy who hung out at the campus nightspots as he watched and waited. Somehow he must have known I was vulnerable. Unfortunately, I did not find out the truth about him until it was too late. I was warned by a few of my sorority sisters when they first noticed him throwing his attention my way. But I didn't listen, because I was flattered to catch the eye of one so smooth and worldly. He had traveled through Europe and was an excellent athlete. Everywhere he went he turned women's heads.

> ⌒ If I had been brave enough to ask my father, I know his answer would have been no.

He had asked me out a few times, but I had turned him down, which made him that much more persistent. I was enjoying his attention from a safe distance. One night I called my mother and shared with her my excitement at the attention of one I considered so far above me. After all, he was smarter, older, and more attractive than I felt I was. I told her he had asked me out, but I wasn't sure if I should go. At some level, I was looking for her to tell me no. I had never asked her permission to go out with any of the other boys I had already dated. She hesitated a moment, then assured me she thought I would be able to handle myself with him. I remember being surprised by her response. I hung up, thinking if my mom says it's okay . . . it's okay. I accepted his next invitation and have lived to regret it. If I had been brave enough to ask my father, I know his answer would have been no. He would have never approved because he would have known right away something was amiss. If I had been wise enough to heed what I knew would be my father's response, I would have been kept safe. But I was not.

This man systematically seduced me over the next few months, and shortly after my nineteenth birthday, I lost my virginity. I had planned to stay the summer in Arizona, but eventually I ran away back home to my parent's house to escape his hold on me. I didn't tell them what had happened. My father didn't approve of him; when he found out I was dating someone nine years older than me, he flipped, but by then it was too late. His hold on me was too strong at that point. I thank God I had a home to run away to, for far too often girls in my situation do not know there is a way of escape.

At the time I was not yet a Christian, nor was my father, but at some level, he knew this arrangement would be dangerous. I believe fathers are equipped to act as the protectors or guardians of virtue of their daughters, and this can happen even if they are not Christians.

But what if you are in a hard place? Your father is no protector. Perhaps he is absent or abusive. Perhaps he violated you sexually himself and is the last person with whom you would feel safe. If this is your story, then it is time to pull rank. If you have no healthy father figure in the natural realm, you still have a heavenly one.

Your heavenly Father would never want to see you violated: He would want you protected and nourished. This means in any given situation you could rightly ask the question, *How would my heavenly Father want me treated? Would He allow this to happen if He knew?* Be certain He would not want you treated as a prostitute. Then, be just as certain He will be there to

> ⌒ *Your heavenly Father would never want to see you violated: He would want you protected and nourished.*

back you up as you take your stand. Don't ever imagine He would make comments like, "You asked for it by being there" . . . He would never say such a thing! He would say, "Get out, get home, and be safe!"

If you are involved with someone who is controlling, and you find that you cannot stand up to him face-to-face, then refuse to meet with him in person. When I was a junior in college, I was seriously involved with another older guy. He was in graduate school, and he had me wrapped around his finger. It was a very unhealthy relationship, but I personally thought he was some sort of prize. My mother and father were very concerned, but I was in Arizona, and they were far away in Indiana. Because they didn't like him, I was even more adamant about making it work.

My mother began to pray in earnest my eyes would be opened and I would somehow escape out of this relationship. After a few weeks of her earnest prayers and petitions, things began to change. Instead of breaking up, we got pinned. But even as I passed my candle, I thought, *Something just isn't right.*

We attended a formal dance together a few nights later, and I just couldn't seem to have any fun. Everywhere we turned, people were congratulating us on our pinning, and I could barely smile. I remember I was drinking heavily, yet I just couldn't seem to get drunk. But my boyfriend wasn't having any problem getting intoxicated, which was something he usually did not do. He was so into control he never wanted to take the chance of losing it by getting drunk. (Of course, he didn't mind my being plastered!) That night, a heavyset girl came over to congratulate him with a kiss, and she actually knocked him over. There he was, flat on his back on the floor, with a woman who was larger than him on top of him, and I had an "Aha" experience!

> *There he was, flat on his back, with a woman who was larger than him on top of him, and I had an "Aha" experience!*

I thought, *What am I doing with this loser!*

I continued to watch them sliding around together on the floor, trying to get up, and I thought, *What did I ever see in this guy?*

I wanted to leave immediately. I wanted to get as far away from him as possible. Unfortunately, everyone in our party of six was drunk except for me, so I had to drive everyone home. When we got to his place, I looked at him and said, "Get out!"

He was stunned and slurred back, "Aren't you coming in and spending the night?"

I told him I was not, in no uncertain terms, and sped off.

Within a half an hour, he was banging on the door of my sorority house, begging to see me. Because he was such a charmer, he talked one of my sorority sisters into coming upstairs to get me so we could talk. He told her how much he loved me, and he didn't want me making any rash decision I'd regret later. She came up and tried to persuade me to come down, but I wasn't interested and told her to send him home. Another sorority sister who was in the hall and heard the whole deal came to my room after the other one left.

She said, "Lisa, this guy is a loser. I haven't seen you happy since you've been involved with him . . . dump him!"

I looked at her and was shocked that she knew my thoughts.

I agreed with her. "You know, I haven't been happy! What am I doing with this guy? I'm giving his pin back! Will you come with me?"

She hugged me and agreed.

We waited until we were certain he was gone, and then we went by his place. I wrapped his fraternity pin in a piece of paper that said, "It's over," and dropped it through the mail slot. Then we returned to our sorority house.

The next morning when I woke up, I was a different person . . . I felt free! At first, I wondered why I felt this way, and then I remembered what I had done the night before. There was no regret. I ran and found my faithful friend and hugged her, saying "I'm free!"

I went down to breakfast with a bounce in my step. While I was eating, there was a phone call for me. I knew it was him so I said, "Take a message." I was feeling more powerful by the minute. I showered and got ready for an interview I had to be a pledge counselor for the next rush.

I got it on the spot. But when I got back to the house, another sorority sister stopped me.

"I saw him at the law library, Lisa. He is so sad . . . he asked me to give you this note."

In the note, he told me he knew I didn't know what I was doing the night before, and as far as he was concerned, he wasn't ready to break up. He wanted me to go out with him that night so we could talk. He planned to call me later to set it up. But there was no way I was going anywhere alone with him. He usually had a way of turning everything around until I was so confused I gave in to whatever he wanted. This was the first time in about nine months I had been able to think straight for myself, and I wasn't willing to give that up. When he called, I wouldn't take his call.

He then began to stalk me on campus. He would go from pleading to yelling to threatening to apologizing and then back to pleading, while I walked along the sidewalk refusing to respond to him. I would enter my classroom, and he would wait until my class let out and then begin the harassment all over again. But in my classes was a wonderful and intelligent, not to mention huge, football player. This guy had watched my situation, and finally decided he'd had more than enough. For the rest of the school year, he walked me to and from class. My ex-boyfriend took one look at him and was smart enough to realize he was only as big as one of this guy's legs! He left me alone until I went home for the summer and was out of his reach.

Abusive, controlling guys will only respect someone or something bigger than themselves. And believe me, like all abusers, they are cowards. You do not owe abusive cowards any explanations. If you decide it is over . . . it is over.

When I went home that summer, my mother shared with me how she had prayed for me to get free. Two months later, I got saved and met John, but I was very afraid about returning to school because my bodyguard had graduated and left school to pursue a job. Who would protect me now? I made this an earnest prayer request. As I feared, I ran into my ex-boyfriend the first week I was back at school. But I was no longer under his influence. I told him I had become a Christian over the summer. He looked startled and told me he

> ∽ *You do not owe abusive cowards any explanations. If you decide it is over . . . it is over.*

had a dream that had happened. He even asked me if I wanted to start a Bible study with him. I thanked him but declined the offer.

I told him I thought it was best for us to stay away from each other completely. He didn't agree, but he only pursued the issue for a few more weeks before he finally left it alone. God had become my bodyguard, and He had even given this guy a dream. I know that had to be from God, because I was the farthest thing from a Christian before I was saved!

Your heavenly Father wants to fight these battles for you as well. He will cover and protect you from harm . . . so let Him.

∽ *Dear Heavenly Father,*

I thank You that You are truly my Father and the ultimate protector and guardian of my virtue. I believe You are always interested in my best interests. I believe I am never alone in any situation. I have angels to protect me and Your Word to keep me. You are a Father I can run to with my deepest, darkest secrets and fears, for You search me and know me. Let me know You as the King who guards and watches over me. I will draw on the safety of Your counsel and not my own. Cover me in the shelter of Your wing.

Love,
Your Daughter

9 *Living Sacrifices*

I remember when the initial revelation hit me that my sexuality was an area of great interest to God. For whatever reason, before this moment I had compartmentalized this area of my life as a *bad* area for *bad* girls. For several years of my life, I had been truly an excellent "bad girl," and so I assumed my sexuality was an area to be left behind, only to be considered as part of my life before I became a Christian. I never wanted to discuss it again if it could at all be ignored and never spoken of with others . . . let alone with God! After all, I reasoned, good Christian girls did not involve themselves in areas of passion. I did not realize the dangers and ignorance of my reasoning. Areas you do not confront head-on will never remain silent. They must be brought to the Cross for a face-off.

> ∼ *Areas you do not confront head-on will never remain silent.*

At that time when I thought of "Christian girls," my mind flashed to images of saints gazing heavenward with the glow of a halo around their heads. I longed to be so other-worldly, but I still struggled with thoughts that were very much earth-bound. I walked a college campus where it was not unusual for me to pass those with whom I'd sinned in various degrees, settings, or manners. Of course, they still thought our past encounters were not only okay but also worth repeating. It was as though their very presence taunted me: "Hi, remember me? I hear you're a Christian now . . . Well, I know better! I know what you're *really* like. You don't fool me. Drop the charade, and lighten up! I liked you better the other way. You're no fun anymore."

This was, of course, only my passing perception, but I had good reason to feel my interpretations were accurate. The first week back at school, in one of my senior group lectures where hundreds of students were present, the student body president himself stood up before the professor walked in and called to me from the front row where he sat, "Hey, Lisa! Is it true what I hear? Are you jumping for Jesus? Well, we won't stand for it! We will kidnap you from the Theta house and make you join us in sex, drugs, and alcohol!"

Every eye in the room was either already fixed on me or searching for my location. Some were even laughing and nodding their heads because they knew what I had been like. My face went hot and red. I was desperately trying to prevent the shaking I felt inside from overtaking my physical body. But the words of Jesus echoed in my heart:

"Whoever acknowledges me before men, I will also acknowledge him before my Father in heaven. But whoever disowns me before men, I will disown him before my Father in heaven." (Matt. 10:32–33)

I rose out of my seat of obscurity in the middle of the terraced auditorium and presented myself to anyone who cared to look. I answered the student-body president, looking him directly in the eye,

"It's true." And then I jumped to prove it!

The president began to laugh, as did the majority of the class. Then I sat down. The professor arrived, and my trial was over. I spent the remainder of the class staring straight ahead, anxious to escape. I knew I had walked out on a limb, but I also knew that was the only safe place for me to be.

I realized, because I had gone out so far, I would be watched. I felt this "watching" acutely as I walked to and from my classes. Previously, the campus had been a haven of friends, fun, and boyfriends. Now it became my crucible of scrutiny and past shame. I had only been saved a mere two weeks before returning to school, and I honestly didn't know how to act.

In addition to all this, I was very confused by the reception I'd received by the other Christians in the sorority house. They seemed to be constantly sending me the same message one way or another: *Calm down, stop talking about Jesus so much, and be a "normal" Christian because you're making everyone uncomfortable.* Those I had thought would encourage me in my pursuit of God were telling me to keep quiet without offering any support. And of course those outside the faith strongly encouraged me to compromise my beliefs.

I did try to quiet down my Christianity somewhat. Little by little, I began to compromise my faith, but I felt as though I died a little each time. I began to think compromise must be the only alternative for young people. The majority of the Christians I met still listened to the same music I had before I became a Christian and attended the same parties I had attended. I, on the other hand, had thrown away the majority of my "B.C." music in my zeal, knowing what the lyrics aroused in me. I tried to attend the same parties after I became a Christian, so everyone would know Christians weren't boring, but I was uncomfortable now that I attended them sober. Without the influence of alcohol, they seemed so stupid. The game was no longer fun for me.

> ⌒ *I began to think compromise must be the only alternative for young people.*

So I began to pursue Christian relationships outside of my sorority house and got involved with Campus Crusade. Through this organization, a lovely sorority sister who'd been the homecoming queen a few years previous took me under her wing with Bible studies and lunch dates. The majority of our time together was spent training me how to witness. We would pray together and then approach individuals or groups on campus. It was a wonderful time of learning.

But I remember something very strange happening one afternoon when we approached a girl reading in the sunshine. As we drew closer, we realized she was reading a Bible and was more than likely already a Christian, but we stopped and spoke with her a moment anyway. When we turned to go, she gave each of us a Scripture. Mine was:

"Arise, my darling, my beautiful one, and come with me.
See! The winter is past; the rains are over and gone." (Song 2:10–11)

I remember thanking her awkwardly as we walked away. My heart was burning within me: What did these words mean? I was determined to spend some time alone with my Bible over the weekend and find out. Sunday morning rose warm and sunny, and I awoke unusually early for a college student. I stole down to the kitchen, where bagels were set out for our breakfast. On Sundays we were on our own for food with the exception of breakfast. I picked up a bagel and was about to place it in my mouth when I heard the Holy Spirit whisper, *Wait.* I actually turned around to see if someone had slipped into the kitchen behind me . . . but I was alone. I wrapped the bagel in a napkin, thinking I should save it until later when I would possibly be a lot hungrier, and left to take it up to my room.

But as I climbed the stairs, I sensed the Holy Spirit instructing me further. I was to save the bagel, go to the convenience store, and buy some grape juice. God was inviting me to share Communion with Him! My excitement built with every step I took. The meaning of the Scripture was already unfolding. He was calling to me and inviting me to come away with Him. I grabbed my Bible and notepad and put them in my backpack with the bagel and some cash. I ran to the store and bought some Welch's, and then slipped off to one of my favorite secluded places on campus. It was a bench almost hidden from view under the canopy of ancient trees. I unpacked all the elements of my divine picnic and opened my Bible. I had been raised in a church where we took Communion each week, and yet I had never received it since becoming a Christian. I wasn't even sure if I could take it alone without the church administering it, so I scanned my Bible to read the teaching on it.

"Take, eat; this is My body which is broken for you; do this in remembrance of Me." In the same manner He also took the cup after supper, saying, "This cup is the new covenant in My blood. This do, as often as you drink it, in remembrance of Me." (1 Cor. 11:24–25 NKJV)

A holy awe settled on me as I realized the meaning of Jesus' words for the first time. This invitation had traveled down through the ages, and

He was now speaking directly to me, telling me: *"This is my body, which is for you."* I was not taking Communion as part of a sterile ritual, but rather in intimate fellowship with the risen Lord and Redeemer of my soul. He had personally invited me to participate in the sacrifice of His body broken on the cross, in the breaking of the bread as a testament of remembrance. He willingly sacrificed that I might live. This was no small thing! He also extended to me the cup of the new covenant purchased with His blood, filled with the crushed produce of the vine. The bread and grape juice sitting before me were symbols of a night long ago and far away, and of a table to which I then drew near by faith. I trembled at the weight of its meaning as I read on.

> *⌒ I was not taking Communion as part of a sterile ritual, but rather in intimate fellowship with the risen Lord and Redeemer of my soul.*

Therefore, whoever eats the bread or drinks the cup of the Lord in an unworthy manner will be guilty of sinning against the body and blood of the Lord. A man ought to examine himself before he eats of the bread and drinks of the cup. For anyone who eats and drinks without recognizing the body of the Lord eats and drinks judgment on himself. (1 Cor. 11:27–29)

This brought me to tears as I remembered the many times I had done this. I had merely gone through the motions without ever truly discerning the Lord's body or examining my own heart. He had laid down His life for me, and I had never once paused to truly judge myself. During Communion time at church, I would look around at everyone else, observing who was there and who wasn't, but I never turned my eyes inward. I even remember staring at statues to see if they were bleeding, all the while neglecting His shed blood for me.

But if we judged ourselves, we would not come under judgment. (1 Cor. 11:31)

I closed my eyes and prayed for the eyes of my understanding to be enlightened and to open up every area of my life. I then invited the Holy Spirit to begin His inspection, allowing the Word of God to act as the judge of my actions and motives. I may have been there for hours, or it may have been minutes. But it was in that time-

> ⟶ *Jesus was asking me to give Him my entire life, and this meant my body as well.*

less place of communion that purity became an issue. As I prayed through the different issues before me, I confessed my sin and felt a cleansing and a release in my heart. Jesus was asking me to give Him my entire life, and this meant my body as well.

> Therefore, I urge you, brothers, in view of God's mercy, to offer your bod-
> ies as living sacrifices, holy and pleasing to God—this is your spiritual act
> of worship. (Rom. 12:1)

We are urged to be pure in view of God's mercy. We are not urged in view of fear, but we are invited to respond in light of the mercy we've already been shown. We are only *urged* when there is great reason or cause. I wanted to grasp the meaning of this Scripture, so I dug deeper and really thought it through. My body was to be presented to God as a living sacrifice. As a Christian, my life is no longer my own for I have been purchased with a price.

This Scripture also promises, God will accept this sacrifice of our lives as holy and pleasing, no matter how sin-scarred and defiled by the world we may be. Now this was a powerful revelation for me. I had never thought of my physical body as capable of acting as an agent of worship before a holy God and being counted as holy and pleasing before Him.

I wanted to hide from my physical self and escape its snares and hold on me, and God was telling me how to accomplish this. If I presented my body to Him for His keeping, and embraced the Cross as a living sacrifice, He would count my offering as righteous for the sake of His Son.

I realized purity is not just a command issued for goodness' sake and then dropped as an impossibility as one progresses from adolescence to adulthood. Instead, it is an act of spiritual worship. Purity was an essential part of denying myself, laying down my life daily to His direction, and taking up my cross. I desired to be bone of His bone and flesh of His flesh, so that His Word might be made flesh in my life.

Matthew Henry's commentary on Romans 12 cites the description of presenting our bodies as living sacrifices as a practical definition of godliness: "our persons and performances, tendered to God through Christ our priest, are as sacrifices of acknowledgment to the honour of God."[1]

The offering is transported to the presence of God through the vehicle of our will. It is in this same manner we draw near in faith just as we pressed in for salvation. Our response to His mercy is to honor the merciful God in our lives. Thus we acknowledge to those around us that we are not our own but have been purchased by another. The commentary continues by stating "God wants your bodies; not your beasts."[2]

I love this admonition: *God wants your bodies; not your beasts.* He doesn't want the dead and bleeding carcasses of animals. He wants hearts beating with love and thanksgiving and bodies consecrated for His purpose and pleasure. David knew this, and although he brought animal sacrifices before the Lord, he always knew what God really wanted all along.

> You do not delight in sacrifice, or I would bring it; you do not take pleasure in burnt offerings. The sacrifices of God are a broken spirit; a broken and contrite heart, O God, you will not despise. (Ps. 51:16–17)

God has always longed for those who can see beyond the veil of religion and the works of the flesh, those who will draw near by faith and worship Him in Spirit and in truth. *He longs for those who want more than just to be good; He desires those who want to be His.*

> ⌒ *God has always longed for those who can see beyond the veil of religion and the works of the flesh.*

Some may argue we don't need to do anything else. Jesus was the final sacrifice, so it's a finished work. But we are not talking about presenting a sin sacrifice. No offering we could bring could satisfy the written statutes against us. Jesus was the Lamb, slain to take away our sins, but He is also the High Priest and our example in all things. Let's look at this relationship together:

> Now if we died with Christ, we believe that we will also live with him. For we know that since Christ was raised from the dead, he cannot die again; death no longer has mastery over him. The death he died, he died to sin once for all; but the life he lives, he lives to God. (Rom. 6:8–10)

By identifying with the death of Christ, we are able to live by virtue of His resurrection. Jesus broke the power of sin and death. Even now, the life He lives He lives for God, not Himself. If anyone could say He had finished the race and run His course, Jesus could. But He doesn't say, "Great! I'm glad that's over with. Now I can live however I want, because it is a finished work." His very life is hid in God, as ours is to be hid in His.

> In the same way, count yourselves dead to sin but alive to God in Christ Jesus. Therefore do not let sin reign in your mortal body so that you obey its evil desires. Do not offer the parts of your body to sin, as instruments of wickedness, but rather offer yourselves to God, as those who have been brought from death to life; and offer the parts of your body to him as instruments of righteousness. For sin shall not be your master, because you are not under law, but under grace. (Rom. 6:11–14)

The phrase "in the same way" means . . . well, *in the same way*. We don't have to shed our blood, because He shed His. But our bodies are to become living sacrifices. We are to live as He did, dead to sin, but alive to God! Sin is not to reign in our bodies . . . God is to reign. We no longer obey our bodies, but God. Obedience is an important idea here. Paul admonishes us not to offer our body parts to sin as instruments of

> ∼ We bring offerings to whatever we obey, and what we obey becomes our master.

wickedness, but to God as instruments of righteousness. Notice, we bring offerings to whatever we obey, and what we obey becomes our master. Obedience is an offering of righteousness, and disobedience is an offering to wickedness. Paul ends with the declaration, "sin is no longer your master." Sin is no longer to receive our offerings or worship, because we escaped the law and are under grace.

Remember in the beginning of Romans 12, we were urged in view of God's mercy, to offer our bodies as living sacrifices. Mercy places us under grace, not the law, and in response to this gracious gift, we follow Christ's pattern of the Cross. We daily yield to God and righteousness rather than to the flesh and wickedness. By an act of our wills, we lay our lives down and present our bodies. Then in faith we are drawn near to pursue the heart of God. This is part of embracing the Cross.

Then he said to them all: "If anyone would come after me, he must deny himself and take up his cross daily and follow me. For whoever wants to save his life will lose it, but whoever loses his life for me will save it." (Luke 9:23–25)

Notice the cross is something we pick up daily. It is not something we do once and then forget about. It is not an ornament about our necks or wrists. It is to be daily emblazoned on our hearts. The priests were to bring offerings before the Lord every day in the temple.

Solomon sacrificed burnt offerings to the LORD, according to the daily requirement for offerings commanded by Moses. (2 Chron. 8:12–13)

The cross is our daily offering. It is not a directive given by the laws of Moses, but from the Lord of life Himself. I am afraid we take His words way too casually, but if we will believe and embrace them, they are living and powerful to deliver and save.

Let's return to the invitation of Communion. What does it mean to be invited to the Communion table of Christ? To answer, we must know

> ⌒ *The cross is our daily offering.*

the meaning of the word *communion*. It is defined as *unity, spiritual union, empathy, close association,* and lastly, *relationship.* The combination of these words gives a portrayal of every woman's deepest desire, to be fully known and yet completely loved.

> Now we see but a poor reflection as in a mirror; then we shall see face to face. Now I know in part; then I shall know fully, even as I am fully known. (1 Cor. 13:12)

To be fully known means a complete and intimate revelation of every flaw and failure, every dream and longing, every fear and hope. It looks beyond action and apprehends the hidden motives of the heart. It sees things we ourselves are blind to. And yet love remains unwaveringly true, even when flaws are in plain sight. Love sees all, because love is the very force behind all true discernment.

An invitation to communion is an offer to be part of a life force much bigger than ourselves. It is an opportunity to eat, drink, and draw our life from another source. We are invited to drink of the living water that quenches our thirst. And even greater, we are invited to not only dine but also to reside, remain, and abide in Him.

> I am the vine; you are the branches. If a man remains in me and I in him, he will bear much fruit; apart from me you can do nothing . . . As the Father has loved me, so have I loved you. Now remain in my love. If you obey my commands, you will remain in my love, just as I have obeyed my Father's commands and remain in his love. (John 15:5, 9–10)

Here is a clear and beautiful illustration of the relationship between Christ and His own. He is the vine from which we draw life, nourishment, and strength. If we remain in Him, we are told we will bear much fruit. What is this fruit?

But the fruit of the Spirit is love, joy, peace, patience, kindness, goodness, faithfulness, gentleness, and self-control. (Gal. 5:22–23)

How do we remain in Him, connected to the vine? John 15:9 tells us if we obey we remain. Obedience to Christ's commands keeps us secure just as He obeyed His Father's commands. Therefore, obedience creates an atmosphere for loving communion.

This is love for God: to obey his commands. And his commands are not burdensome. (1 John 5:3)

I know I have emphasized obedience very heavily in this chapter, but I believe it is a virtue we do not speak of enough. It is one Jesus spoke of repeatedly. Obedience is mentioned sixty-seven times in the New Testament alone. All of us have been disobedient at one time or another, and we know how it moves us away from a consciousness of righteousness and into a sin-consciousness, which separates us from Him.

I want to invite you to press beyond the veil of the flesh and shed the shadow that would cross between you and your Prince. We are invited to . . .

Lay aside every weight, and the sin which so easily ensnares us, and let us run with endurance the race that is set before us, looking unto Jesus, the author and finisher of our faith. (Heb. 12:1–2 NKJV)

God has written your love story and promised to walk with you through the process, feed you and sustain you for the journey. I want you to join Him now in communion. As you begin this journey of feeding on His Word and His faithfulness, allow Him to be your source of life and empowerment as well.

⌒ *Dear Heavenly Father,*

I come to You in the name of Jesus. I accept Your invitation to eat at Your table, to feast on Your love and faithfulness. Just as Jesus presented Himself as a sacrifice for sin at the Last Supper, I now embrace the mercy of God and follow His example. I present my body as a living sacrifice, holy and acceptable in Your sight, because I have been washed in the blood of Your precious Son. No longer will I yield my body to disobedience and my members to sin. I present them anew to You. I thank You for the life of Christ coursing through my veins. Jesus, You are the Living Vine, and I am a branch. I thank You for the ability to bear fruit in You. You are my life and strength, and I now draw from that well that never runs dry. I lay aside every weight and sin that might try to hold me back. Let me realize Your love as never before. Help me to love You in all I am. I embrace life in the Spirit, which is to daily deny myself, take up my cross, and follow You.

Love,

Your Daughter

10 Breaking the Curse

I awoke with a start. My heart was racing, and my breath labored in forced gasps. I had pulled myself awake to escape the grip of yet another horrible nightmare. I opened my eyes slowly and looked up at the ceiling where the gray, early-morning light shone and realized that John was not in bed with me. I listened for his movements somewhere else in our apartment, but I heard nothing except the neighbor moving around upstairs. I called for him anyway.

"John!"

My voice sounded frightened and childish, even to my own ears. Its tone brought back memories of my childhood when, after a frightening dream, I would call to my mother . . . first in a whisper, then when I was certain nothing in my room would pounce on me, louder and louder until I progressed to a full-fledged yell, and Mom would come running. But this time there was no answer.

I called John's name again as I sat up to look at the clock, noticing I was drenched in sweat. This time my voice echoed back a little quieter, a little calmer, almost as a question, but I already knew for certain by the lateness of the hour that John was gone. How could I have slept through his morning routine when I was having such a restless and disturbing dream?

I tried to shake the clammy shroud of it off of me, for it could become a fear that lingered far into my day. Over the past few months I had been experiencing a recurring nightmare. It was one I'd known as a child. Its cold grip would grab me perhaps once a year, and then it would fade away. But now it was tenacious in its pursuit and rapidly increased its visits from yearly haunts to monthly interruptions to weekly turmoil, finally progressing until its presence dominated my rest nightly.

In the last few weeks, I had become afraid to sleep, afraid to close my eyes in rest, because in the dark of night I fought my dream alone. John and I were newly married, and each night I had him pray with me that the dream would not visit again as I slept. Each night I fell asleep with his arms pulled tightly around me to ward off any would-be sleep intruders, but as John's body relaxed and he slipped into sleep, I felt the whispers of fear draw near. I would quote Psalm 91 over and over until finally I succumbed to the weight of sleep.

This sleep would begin in a happy dream, then move easily from that to another, as if changing channels on a television. Then, the channel would be stuck, and a dream would begin from which I couldn't escape. It varied a little each time although its theme stayed consistent, and I always recognized its story line as soon as it began. Even in my sleep I would protest . . . *not this dream again! I hate this dream.*

In the dream, I always started out in my parents' home. I would leave my childhood home, happy and excited to travel to a friend's house, to school, or to the store (where I was going was never the issue). Then suddenly, everything would change. I'd turn the corner, and the sky would loom gray before me. As I stepped into the twilight, I would see the black of nightfall in the close distance. Behind me, just a few steps away, the sun was still shining. For a moment, I was poised between day and night and realized the darkness was not a function of time but of the presence of a dark or evil dimension. I would turn and begin to run back toward the sunlight and home. But it seemed as though I was trapped in the gray and darkening twilight. I ran with great effort but made very little progress, for the sunshine stayed just out of my reach. My body moved

> ⌒ *For a moment, I was poised between day and night and realized the darkness was not a function of time but of the presence of evil.*

in slow motion as though moving through something thick. While still running, I would look back over my shoulder into the deeper shadowy darkness beyond the gray.

That is where I would see them walking . . . always walking. Three shadowy figures approaching with ease, shortening the distance between us. With each step, they decreased the very gap I could not widen with all my running. I would turn my face away from them in horror and strain even harder to break free from the gray mist, but my frantic attempts at progress remained slow in comparison to their steady gait. I could see my house in the distance, but it was as though it was a hundred miles away. I could not seem to close the distance.

I would look back again and find the shadowy figures gaining on me, and soon they were close enough for me to see more than just an outline of them. The forms were three men, following me, each dead but walking, each in a different stage of decay. One was just dead; he moved with an absence of life. The next was partially decayed, and the last was barely more than a skeleton with hair. Their clothes mirrored their stages of decay as well; one was fully dressed, the next was dressed in torn garments, and the skeleton's shredded garments looked like wretched rags on masts of bone. They walked shoulder to shoulder, in perfect stride with one another. Without a word or a glance toward one another, they moved with one purpose: They were after me.

In the dream all this would register in one backward glance as I strained forward against the shadows. As they grew closer, my movements became clumsier as I became more frightened and wild with panic. I would trip or stumble on the very sidewalk I used daily as a child. Finally, I would begin to yell at them while still running, because I realized I would not be successful in outrunning them by myself.

"Who are you? Go away! You're dead. Leave me alone!"

They would never answer me, nor hesitate for even a moment. It was as though they were deaf to my voice. They were driven by the voice of some unseen commander. I would continue running, and they would continue walking, closing in on me with each step. Then suddenly, they would be too close, too terrible to look at, and I would begin to throw stones or sticks their way, but nothing slowed them down. After all, why would any of this hurt them when they were dead already? My futile attempts only slowed down my own forward progress.

Then it would happen. They were upon me, reaching out to grab me. The terror was so overwhelming that I would jolt awake.

I left my bedroom and wandered into the kitchen of our small apartment. So many questions stirred in my mind that I couldn't answer them all.

Why was this happening when I was claiming Scriptures and praying? Wasn't God more powerful than this dream? Why didn't He stop it? As a Christian, how could I have this little power and protection?

The phone rang, and I almost jumped out of my skin. I snatched the phone from the receiver.

"Hello?" I answered, a little edgy.

"Hi, honey. I didn't want to wake you when I left. You were sleeping so soundly, and I know you've had some rough nights, so I wanted you to be able to sleep in," John said.

"I wish you would have wakened me. I had the dream again."

"I'm sorry. I would have if I'd known."

"John, why doesn't it stop? We prayed last night!" I questioned.

"I don't know," John answered honestly.

I could tell by his tone he was almost as frustrated as I was.

We talked awhile longer, then hung up, and I wandered into the living room to read my Bible. But I felt as though my mind was in a fog as I fought to stay awake and attempted to focus on the meaning of the words I read. I felt as though I was again trying to escape my dream. The heavy hand of sleep was weighing me down as well, and I kept moving into more and more uncomfortable positions to keep myself awake, but my brain fog wasn't lifting.

I prayed, "God, please show me something or someone who can help me!"

Almost as an immediate answer, I thought of a man who had adopted me as his "daughter" when I moved to Dallas. I got up from the sofa and called him from the kitchen. It just so happened that he was available, and I poured out the whole story through tears to him, closing with my complaint, "I can't believe as a Christian that this is life, and life more abundantly!"

He told me that he agreed with me and explained that he was going to send me three tapes he wanted me to listen to when I was alone, and after listening to them, I was to call him so we could talk. I made him promise to send them soon, and we hung up. For the first time, I felt a glimmer of hope. I opened the curtains to invite in the Texas sunshine and hopped in the shower.

The nightly terror of the dream continued, but after a few short days had passed, the package of tapes arrived. I was as excited as if they were a birthday gift. I went into our dining room and set up a makeshift study complete with notepad, Bible, highlighter, and cassette player. I prayed, "Father, let me know the truth, and may it set me free! Open my eyes to see, my ears to hear, and my heart to believe. In Jesus' name. Amen."

I plugged in the first tape. The recording was poor, and I found myself straining to hear the muffled words. It was an older man teaching on things I had never even heard of, but at the same time it was as though he knew just what I was wrestling with. He began by explaining that most Christians are afraid to discuss spiritual warfare because we believe to do so would just make the evil forces stronger. As a result, we do not stand fast in our resistance of evil, but we back down in fear. He explained that Satan is already operating at full strength, and by exposing his deeds of darkness, we diminish his power, not increase it. He explained that Satan is

> ∼ *Most Christians are afraid to discuss spiritual warfare because we believe to do so would make the evil forces stronger.*

a legalist who operates as the accuser of the brethren. He is to be resisted steadfastly in the faith and with the sword of God's Word. Then the speaker went in-depth into a teaching on generational sins and curses. The first two tapes were comprised of teaching, and the third provided a time of prayer. I read along in my Bible and saw truths that now seemed glaringly obvious, but they were nevertheless ones I had previously overlooked or discounted.

Now to you, these may not seem like new truths, but back in 1982, they were pretty radical concepts. One of the most powerful and dynamic truths I learned that day that I want to share with you is the principle of appropriating the promises of God in our lives.

> For no matter how many promises God has made, they are "Yes" in Christ. And so through him the "Amen" is spoken by us to the glory of God. (2 Cor. 1:20)

This is an awesome promise. Regardless of the number or magnitude of God's promises, His answer is always yes in Christ. Let me illustrate this with an Old Testament example. God

> ⌒ *Regardless of the number or magnitude of God's promises, His answer is always yes in Christ.*

set before Moses and the children of Israel blessings and curses. The congregation, with their pronouncement of "amen," affirmed the list of blessings after each reading. The word *amen* means "so be it." An example of this is found in Deuteronomy:

> See, I am setting before you today a blessing and a curse—the blessing if you obey the commands of the LORD your God that I am giving you today; the curse if you disobey the commands of the LORD your God. (Deut. 11:26–28)

Under the Law, every blessing had a curse attached to it if the command of the Lord was broken. But Christ broke the power of the Law.

> Christ redeemed us from the curse of the law by becoming a curse for us, for it is written: "Cursed is everyone who is hung on a tree." He redeemed us in order that the blessing given to Abraham might come to the Gentiles through Christ Jesus, so that by faith we might receive the promise of the Spirit. (Gal. 3:13–14)

In Christ, we inherit the blessings of Abraham. To receive the blessing of Moses, we would have to be the seed of Israel, but the blessing of Abraham is extended to the Gentiles. In Christ, those outside of the Law were brought in on a new and living covenant through faith. So in Christ, we hear "yes"—not an "if you keep the law, yes," but an "in Christ, yes." Notice again our part in 2 Corinthians 1:20:

> For no matter how many promises God has made, they are "Yes" in Christ. And so *through him the "Amen" is spoken by us* to the glory of God. (emphasis added)

We say "amen," or "let it be so!" We look into the Word, and then by faith draw near, so the Word can be made flesh in our lives. We appropriate the Word in our lives by faith. We submit our wills and thus our lives to His truth by saying, "I receive Your engrafted Word into my heart. Let it have its way in my life."

When the Word convicts us, we repent and submit to its counsel. When the Word challenges us, we say, "I believe . . . Lord, help my unbelief!" We declare, "May the Word of the Lord endure forever, and be glorified in my life!"

That day, as I listened to those cassette tapes, I saw very clearly through the mirror of the Word, areas of my life where I needed to renounce my former involvement in darkness and confess the sins of my fathers before me. I could see the dark shadow of curses in my life, the lives of my parents, and my grandparents. At the same time, I saw the blessing of Christ hovering over me and future generations, just waiting for someone to stand in the gap and say, "Yes!" I felt such an awesome responsibility as I knelt before the Lord, confessed, and renounced my sins and the generational sins of my family. I felt as though I was echoing the words of Hezekiah:

> *I saw the blessing of Christ hovering over me and future generations, just waiting for someone to stand in the gap and say, "Yes!"*

Now I intend to make a covenant with the LORD, the God of Israel, so that his fierce anger will turn away from us. (2 Chron. 29:10)

Hezekiah had just confessed the error of his fathers and then declared his commitment to God. I was definitely from a long line of heathens with a long list of infractions. Of course, I was no more able to confess their sins individually than I had been able to confess my own when I acknowledged myself as a sinner before God, but there were some specific things of which I knew I was guilty.

- Occult involvement through astrology, as well as through other questionable books, toys, and movies

- Drug and alcohol abuse

- Sexual sin

I had not realized even a casual association with these things is potentially lethal. I remembered reading a book of my parents which profiled each astrological sign. I also used to like to read my horoscope—even though it was just for a laugh, I did in fact read them. I had received a Ouija board for Christmas one year and played with it a lot until it scared me by moving by itself. Before becoming a Christian, I loved to read horror stories and was fascinated with anything supernatural. Of course, I now believe this was actually an underlying hunger for the things of God that I sought to satisfy in an inappropriate way, but nevertheless it had placed me under a curse rather than a blessing.

My grandmother and father were alcoholics, and I myself had started drinking at the age of fourteen and did not stop drinking regularly until I was twenty-one. I had tried marijuana a few times and experimented with cocaine while in college. All of these were acts of rebellion and opened the door in my life to curses rather than blessings.

There were other things I noticed as I looked closer at the generations that preceded me. My grandmother had had cancer, my mother had had cancer, and I had had cancer. Three generations. My great-grandmother was married twice. My grandmother divorced and then remarried her first husband, and then divorced him again, and then married her second husband, and then divorced him and married her third, who died when he suffered a heart attack during a heated argument. My father's mother had been married twice. My mother and father had divorced, remarried, then divorced, and my father finally left for another woman whom he never bothered to marry. My grandmother had miscarried one child and almost died in childbirth with another. My mother had miscarried three children between my birth and the birth of my brother. Why was all of this happening and repeating itself?

> "The LORD, the LORD, the compassionate and gracious God, slow to anger, abounding in love and faithfulness, maintaining love to thousands, and forgiving wickedness, rebellion and sin. Yet he does not leave the guilty unpunished; he punishes the children and their children for the sin of the fathers to the third and fourth generation." (Ex. 34:6–7)

I felt as though these things would continue to repeat their process in my life, in my marriage, and if allowed, in my children yet unborn, unless something was done. God was showing me how to stop the progression of these curses. When I looked at this Scripture, I saw both a reason and a promise. I was the third and sometimes the fourth generation in these cycles of sins. That was definitely a reason, but in another version of this I found my promise:

> I, the LORD your God, am a jealous God, punishing the children for the sin of the fathers to the third and fourth generation of those who hate me, but showing love to a thousand [generations] of those who love me and keep my commandments. (Ex. 20:5–6)

I wanted to be the beginning of a thousand generations who loved God and kept His commandments. This was my opportunity to repent of the sins of previous generations and strike a covenant with the merciful God. He was just waiting for me to call upon His name so that He might extend His love to a thousand generations. I was trembling with excitement when I realized the impact the choice of covenant and obedience would have on my life and the lives that passed through me.

> *I was trembling with excitement when I realized the impact the choice of covenant and obedience would have on my life and the lives that passed through me.*

Through the tapes, my eyes were opened to yet another form of bondage of which I had previously been unaware. It was the principle of soul ties, and I had some really unhealthy ones that needed severing. I believe that we can confront areas of captivity without overexalting their intricacies. Jesus cast out devils and set people free without ever conducting a demonology seminar. When He saw chains, He broke them; when He saw demons, He drove them out; when He saw sickness and infirmities, He healed them; when He saw those bound by sin, He forgave and then empowered them to go and sin no more.

I love Jesus because He is so real, so relevant, and so practical. He knew I was bound, and so He placed in my hands truths with the power to set me free. I, in turn, now place these same truths in your hands. Their powers are undiminished, for truth is no respecter of persons, but a liberator of all who will turn and honor it.

So, what is a soul tie? In very simple terms, for we are to be like children when it comes to these things, it occurs when our souls become knit to another. Now obviously, this can be both a good and a bad thing. A mother's soul is knit to her infant son's. But as he grows and becomes a man, the relationship with his mother must change so he can give his heart to his wife. A husband's soul should be knit to his bride's so that the two may become one flesh. He leaves his mother and father and cleaves to his wife. These are good and healthy ties that bind and knit our hearts together in love. Healthy ties like this can also be forged in friendships. David and Jonathan had just such a relationship. We find it described in the following verses:

> After David had finished talking with Saul, Jonathan became one in spirit
> with David, and he loved him as himself . . . And Jonathan made a covenant
> with David because he loved him as himself. (1 Sam. 18:1, 3)

> Jonathan said to David, "Go in peace, for we have sworn friendship with each
> other in the name of the LORD, saying, 'The LORD is witness between you and
> me, and between your descendants and my descendants forever.'" (1 Sam. 20:42)

This alliance and knitting in friendship preserved David's life and
later the lives of the descendants of Jonathan. These two men bound
themselves together in covenant even at the expense of their own comfort or positions. Jonathan yielded his royal right to the throne because
of his love for David and his recognition of God's hand on David's life.
I am certain that you have such a friendship in your life. It may be with
a sister or close friend. There is an unspoken knowing between you. I
definitely have it with my boys—there are times when I don't just know
what they are thinking; I feel it as well.

So far, we have discussed the healthy ties between friends and parents. But let's look deeper at the ties forged between husbands and wives.
This tie began with Adam and Eve. It is the mystery of two becoming
one . . . one man, one woman, one flesh. Jesus described it this way:

> "But at the beginning of creation God 'made them male and female.' For this
> reason a man will leave his father and mother and be united to his wife, and
> the two will become one flesh. So they are no longer two, but one. Therefore
> what God has joined together, let man not separate." (Mark 10:6–9)

This is obviously a reference to the original plan in the book of
Genesis, the purity of purpose from the very beginning. Husbands and
wives are no longer two but one. This merger is powerful and life giving.
First, souls are knit together in love. Then their love progresses to a
covenant of pledging and making vows before God. This culminates in
sexual union, when their bodies are knit together. Eventually, the seed

of the man is planted in the womb of the woman, and life comes forth.

They are joined mentally, physically, and spiritually through sexual union. This is the highest level of agreement, because it occurs on all three levels of intimacy. Before this union, each individual is complete by himself or herself, but when the union takes place, the two are no longer separate but one. They are now stronger together than either could be if separate. This is not a diminishing but a completion. This also explains why it is so devastating when two that are one go through the betrayal of adultery or divorce. It is a rending or tearing of their souls. Only husbands and wives should be joined on all three levels this way.

This knitting of souls can occur sexually outside of marriage as well as in a marriage relationship. When a man and woman have a sexual relationship, there is a sexual soul tie forged between them. In other words, there really is no such thing as casual sex. The encounter leaves both parties changed—not just in their souls but physically as well. I heard an interesting fact recently on a TV show about AIDS: When you have sex with someone, you are really also having sex biologically with them and everyone else they've slept with for the last seven years. The physical residue of these encounters remains intact for a full seven years!

In Genesis, we find an encounter between Dinah (the daughter of Leah and Jacob) and a prince.

> *There really is no such thing as casual sex. The encounter leaves both parties changed.*

And when Shechem the son of Hamor the Hivite, prince of the country, saw her, he took her and lay with her, and violated her. His soul was strongly attracted to Dinah the daughter of Jacob, and he loved the young woman and spoke kindly to the young woman. So Shechem spoke to his father Hamor, saying, "Get me this young woman as a wife." (Gen. 34:2–5 NKJV)

After this, Shechem's soul was knit to Dinah, and he wanted her for his wife. Notice it said he "violated her." His desire to marry her afterwards did not cancel the violation before. Sex outside of marriage will

> ⌒ *His desire to marry her afterwards did not cancel the violation before. Sex outside of marriage will always be a violation, even if you're engaged.*

always be a violation, even if you're engaged. If he had taken her as his bride first, and then laid with her, then no such violation would have occurred. If this whole scenario had been turned upside down, everything would have been different. But let's examine the order in which it happened: He saw her, was physically attracted to her, took her, lay with her, violated her, and then his soul was attracted to her. He loved her, spoke kindly to her, and then he asked his father for her as a wife. He seemed to have everything backwards.

If Shechem had first spoken with his father and asked for her as his bride, everything would have been different. I wonder if, when he spoke tenderly to Dinah, he said, "Don't worry. Everything will be all right, I'm going to marry you and make this wrong right." It is interesting that we are not given any record of Dinah's feeling in the whole matter. Was she raped or seduced? Did she even want to be his bride? Because of the way things happened, we get the impression that she was merely a victim, not participating in the things being done to her and the decisions being made without her. When unhealthy soul ties form, there is control and fear rather than union and fellowship. And in unhealthy ties, women tend to be the victims more often than not. Of course, this story doesn't have a happy ending; the prince is killed, and Dinah ends up alone.

Ideally, you are to be united sexually with only one person because sex is reserved for the union of two in the covenant of marriage. There sex is not a violation, but the very opposite. When we violate something, we dishonor, desecrate, or defile it.

Sex outside of marriage dishonors marriage, each participant, and God, but sex within the covenant of marriage honors God and the husband and wife. This is why we are admonished to keep the marriage bed holy.

Marriage should be honored by all, and the marriage bed kept pure, for God will judge the adulterer and all the sexually immoral. (Heb. 13:4)

We honor our marriages by remaining pure and reserved for our future mates. We honor our marriage beds after the wedding by never allowing others in (adultery) or anything else to detract from the beauty of sexual intimacy (such as pornography, masturbation, perversion, or impurity).

Well, this was all a news flash for me. I had quite a colorful past, and now that I was married, ugly faces and memories from my checkered past were rearing their heads at me. John and I would be alone together, and I would suddenly experience a terrifying flashback of an image in some horrible X-rated movie I had seen five years earlier in college. Or, I would find myself shutting down sexually with shame from memories of past sexual encounters I had with a former boyfriend. It was terrible. Of course, none of this type of thing had bothered me when I was a single heathen, but now that I was a married Christian, it was like a sexual time bomb.

When I should have been able to give myself freely to my husband with total abandonment, I found myself tethered to the past. I was bound in marriage when I had been previously

> ⌒ *When I should have been able to give myself freely I found myself tethered to the past.*

uninhibited in fornication. How horrible! John deserved all of me, and I was no longer capable of sexual freedom because of my previous violations. I wrestled with impure thoughts, images, comparisons, and shame. I struggled against them, but it seemed to be to no avail . . . that is, until I learned about the power of breaking soul ties and renouncing generational sins. Let's look at a New Testament Scripture that addresses this:

> Do you not know that your bodies are members of Christ himself? Shall I then take the members of Christ and unite them with a prostitute? Never! Do you not know that he who unites himself with a prostitute is one with her in body? For it is said, "The two will become one flesh." (1 Cor. 6:15–16)

I am not calling my ex-boyfriends prostitutes, but the principle is the same here. I had been one with them, and now I had a covenant with another. With each joining and separation, my soul had been fragmented until I was no longer whole but broken sexually. When you are broken sexually, it makes it incredibly difficult for you to give yourself completely to your husband, because you are not complete anymore.

> ⌒ When you are broken sexually, it makes it incredibly difficult for you to give yourself completely because you are not complete.

This same principle makes it very difficult for sexually broken or violated women to stand strong in the face of temptation. They have a hard time saying no even when they want to. They are overwhelmed with either lust or guilt, and often both, which makes it nearly impossible for them to resist sexual advances. They become victims and a magnet for sexual abuse and promiscuity. Things are done to them, or they find themselves inflamed with lust because of past encounters with other partners. But the impossible without God becomes the possible with Him.

In order to walk in purity, we must be whole, and only God can restore us to wholeness where there has been brokenness. Only God can restore honor to our sexuality when there's been violation and dishonor. Only God can take the impure and defiled and make it holy and pure again. Only God can give us beauty for the ashes we bring Him.

I determined that day to set apart some time and collect all my burnt offerings of sexual sin and shame. The following evening I had my opportunity to present them to the Lord. John would be gone, and I would be free to really spend the time I needed alone before the Lord in prayer. I believe God will bring these issues to our attention when we are ready to confront them, and I was ready! Perhaps you hold this book in your hand as His invitation to do the same.

We have a faithful and compassionate High Priest who knows us intimately. He is willing to use His sword to sever anything that holds you back from Him. He wants every unhealthy soul tie severed so only what is healthy will remain. He will send His Word to heal and restore your soul. His angels will go where you now fear to tread and return every broken fragment of your soul back to you.

Are not all angels ministering spirits sent to serve those who will inherit salvation? (Heb. 1:14)

Angels are guardians of our souls. They are not to be worshiped, but they are definitely involved with those who inherit salvation. There is no reason to fear their involvement because it is commissioned by God Himself.

I want to invite you to set aside some time for prayer to allow God to accomplish His purification of your life. He who promises is faithful. He will pull you out of the miry clay and set your feet on solid rock. But you must position your heart for Him to do this in your life. This is not something to be taken casually. You may want to even fast a meal and spend some time in worship before proceeding. I want you to be truly sensitive to the leading of the Holy Spirit as He moves you gently through this process and helps you renounce every dark and shadowy stronghold of the enemy. And what about my nightmare? I never had it again after I renounced these things in prayer.

> ⌒ *He will pull you out of the miry clay and set your feet on solid rock. But you must position your heart.*

Please take a moment to pause and set time apart before proceeding. It could be right now; if so, please make sure you are alone or with only a close friend or prayer partner, for you will need to speak out loud your petitions, renouncements, and your response, "yes and amen."

As much as possible I have constructed this prayer by combining Scriptures, for the Word is the sharp and powerful, two-edged sword of the Spirit. I have included references at the close of this chapter for your further study.

〜 Dear Heavenly Father,

I come before You in the name of Your precious Son, Jesus; I enter Your gates with thanksgiving and come into Your courts with praise. I am overwhelmed by Your gracious mercy and love for me, and I thank You in advance for the mighty work of redemption You have wrought in my life.

Now I intend to make a covenant with the Lord, the God of Israel. You are the Lord, the God of heaven and earth, the great and awesome God, who keeps His covenant of love with those who love Him and obey His commands. Let Your ear be attentive and Your eyes open to hear the prayer of Your servant. I confess my sins and the sins of my father's house, every transgression we have committed against You. Forgive us, for we have acted very wickedly toward You. We have been covered with shame because we sinned against You. But You, Lord, our God, are merciful and forgiving, even though we have rebelled against You and have not obeyed the Lord our God or kept the laws He gave us through His servants, the prophets. We ask You to circumcise our hearts and roll away the sin, shame, and reproach of our sojourn in Egypt from us.

I confess and renounce my sin and the sins of my forefathers, for any and all involvement in the occult, witchcraft, or divination. (Pause here, and stay sensitive to add anything the Holy Spirit brings to your attention to specifically renounce before continuing. This may include, but certainly is not limited to, astrology, séances, horror movies, games, books, etc.) I renounce my involvement in these things and break their curse off my life and off the lives of my children, their children, and their children's children.

I confess and renounce my sin and/or the sins of my forefathers in the area of drug and alcohol abuse. Father, close any door this may have opened in the spirit realm to sin, bondage, or oppression. I renounce my involvement with (specifically call the drugs out by name, if applicable), and I break the power of their curse off my life and off the lives of my children, their children, and their children's children.

Father, I confess and renounce my sin and the sins of my forefathers for any and all involvement in sexual sin and all impurity, perversion, incest, and promiscuity. (Be sensitive here to specifically name the sins you are renouncing.

Speak them out before Him without shame. There is nothing hidden—He knows each of them already and longs to remove their weight of guilt and shame from you. Then, when you are ready, proceed.)

Father, take the sword of Your Spirit and sever every ungodly sexual soul tie between me and . . . (listen to the Holy Spirit, and speak each name out as you hear it. It is quite possible the names may even be of those with whom you did not have intercourse, but with whom you were sexually or emotionally involved in a way that should be reserved for your husband or Savior alone.)

After speaking each name out individually, pray this:

Father, release Your angels to retrieve the fragments of my soul from these men (or women). Restore them to me by Your Spirit so that I might be whole, holy, and set apart for Your pleasure.

Father, I renounce the hold of every perverted and promiscuous image. Forgive me for allowing vile and perverted images before my eyes. I make a covenant according to Psalm 101:3, and I will guard the issues of my heart by way of the gateway of my eyes. I will not allow any vile thing before my eyes. I renounce every unclean spirit and command it and its influence to leave my life.

Father, wash me in the cleansing blood of Jesus, for it alone has the power to cleanse and atone. I consecrate myself now as Your temple; by the power of Your Holy Spirit, remove all defilement of the spirit, soul, and flesh from this sanctuary. Fill me to overflowing with the indwelling of Your Holy Spirit. Open my eyes to see, my ears to hear, and my heart to receive all that You have for me. I am Yours. Have Your way in my life.

> *Love,*
> *Your Daughter*

References: Psalm 100:4, 2 Chronicles 29:10–11, Nehemiah 1:5–7, Daniel 9:8–10, Joshua 5:9, Matthew 10:34, Hebrews 4:12, 2 Chronicles 29:5–6

11 *Chosen by a Passionate, Holy God*

Do you realize a passionate, holy God is pursuing you? He is waiting and watching for you to glance His way. He longs for you to read the love notes He's written. He prays you will return His advances. He wants to bring you out of a world of darkness and into His glorious world of light. He longs to snatch you from the arms of faithless lovers to and bring you into His faithful, everlasting arms. He delivers you from the hard taskmasters and cruel bondages of Egypt and instead shows you His tender love and mercy.

> ⌒ *He longs to snatch you from the arms of faithless lovers to and bring you into His faithful, everlasting arms.*

He doesn't rescue us from Egypt just to bring us to the promised land, He ultimately wants to bring us to Himself. The promises in the Old Testament are merely an earthly shadow of things to come. Too often, we think like the children of Israel thought. We are so relieved to be saved and to escape judgment, we forget His ultimate purpose in salvation is restoration to Himself. Beloved, redemption is so much more than fire and life insurance!

However, I understand why you may have looked at redemption in this way. How many of us have heard the question, "If you died tonight, do you know for certain where you would go?" The purpose of the question is to get the audience to ask themselves, "Do I know for sure that I would go to heaven?" If they don't, they have an opportunity to pray and assure their eternal positions. But salvation is not just a destination after death; it is a way of life and life more abundantly. Hear God's deepest desire and purpose in liberating Israel from Egypt:

> You yourselves have seen what I did to Egypt, and how I carried you on eagles' wings and brought you to myself. (Ex. 19:4)

I love the beauty and power of this verse. The mighty King of heaven swoops down to valiantly rescue His children after four hundred years of slavery. In the process, He strikes Egypt, the most powerful nation in the world, and reduces it to a humiliated wreck. The Israelite slaves spoil the Egyptians of their silver and gold.

Who among us does not long to be swept away from this world's harsh captivity and carried to the mountain of God, where there is safety and intimate fellowship beyond compare? I am afraid more people than you might realize do not truly have this longing in their hearts. Though many welcome the escape from bondage and judgment, they really do not make the connection: It is all about becoming His. If we no longer belong to this present world, then whose are we?

> "Speak to the *entire assembly* of Israel and say to them: 'Be holy because I, the LORD your God, am holy.'" (Lev. 19:2, emphasis added)

Holiness is not just a job description for ministers or a suggested alternative lifestyle, but it is a command for *all* who assemble before the holy God. We are to be holy, for *He* is holy. We are not asked merely to act holy or to appear holy; we are invited to *be* holy. To *be* something means it becomes part of our essence or life force. Our spirits direct how we live, so we are to be filled and led by the Spirit, which is holy, or the Holy Spirit.

> ⌒ *Holiness is not just a job description for ministers, but it is a command for all who assemble before the holy God.*

This includes our private interactions as well as our public behavior, but I want to focus on the realm of the unseen and private. To *be* something means it defines your very existence. We can *act* holy but not *be* holy; we can *look* holy but not *be* holy. This is not just an old-fashioned Old Testament directive. We are admonished under the New Testament covenant of grace to be holy as well.

> But just as he who called you is holy, so be holy in all you do; for it is written: "Be holy, because I am holy." (1 Peter 1:15–16)

If you look closely at this New Testament reference to the Leviticus admonishment, it is actually more specific, instructing to be holy in *all* we do, for God is holy in *all* He is.

What does it mean to *be holy*? This next Scripture lends us some additional insight:

> You are to be holy to me because I, the LORD, am holy, and I have *set you apart* from the nations to be my own. (Lev. 20:26, emphasis added)

God told Israel to be holy because they'd been set apart from the nations to be His. In essence, God said to them, "Set yourselves apart for Me, because I have chosen you as My own. Choose Me, for I've already chosen you." Israel was chosen from among the host of nations to be His. Where do the Gentiles fit in? When were we chosen?

> For he chose us in him before the creation of the world to be holy and blameless in his sight. (Eph. 1:4)

Before He even beheld us, we were chosen in Him. In Christ we were chosen, not from among the nations, but before the very creation of the world. It would appear we were already on His mind when He created the earth. We were chosen by God in Christ, the Lamb slain before the foundations of the earth. We were destined to be holy and blameless in Christ.

What does it mean to be holy in His sight? In Christ, we were made holy, or set apart for Him, for His pleasure, purpose, and glory. Before, we were aliens to the promises, for those outside the nation of Israel could not be holy or set apart. Gentiles had to keep all the laws and statues in order to enter the covenant.

But today, the curtain has been rent in two. The statutes that were against us have been nailed to Christ's cross, and we are no longer separated from God (Col. 2:14). Holiness is not God's asking us to be "good"; it is an invitation to be "His." I did not marry John in order to escape being single and to have children . . . I married John so I could be *his*. Because of our covenant relationship, we share a lot of things in common. We share secrets, children, finances,

> ⌒ *Holiness is not God's asking us to be "good"; it is an invitation to be "His."*

cars, fellowship, a home, a bed, etc. But there are places in my life John can never touch because they are reserved for God, just as there are places and needs I can never meet in John's life because they are for God alone. Every woman is destined to belong to her Prince, and there are places in her life reserved only for Him.

To be holy is to be set apart, in our spirits, souls, and physical bodies, for Him. We set ourselves apart by first responding to His call, then by submitting our wills to His Word by asking the Holy Spirit to guide us.

> But you are a chosen people, a royal priesthood, a holy nation, a people belonging to God, that you may declare the praises of him who called you out of darkness into his wonderful light. (1 Peter 2:9–10)

We are chosen as royal priests of His holy nation. We belong to God, and therefore declare His praises to this world out of our love and gratitude for His death that delivered us from a world of darkness into His glorious light. I remember that in college, after being initiated into a sorority, we sisters all had the thrill of belonging to something so much bigger than ourselves, and we sang the praises of our house at all the school functions. If we were this happy about a social club, how much more should we praise God, who welcomed us into His kingdom? First Peter tells us what our position in Christ is: We are chosen, royal, holy priests.

In the Old Testament, priests were entrusted with the responsibility of offering sacrifices, and royal priests bring their sacrifices before their royal king. As priests, what is our sacrifice? It is a life that praises Him in word, deed, and appearance. To further understand this, let's look at Aaron:

> Then they made the plate of the holy crown of pure gold, and wrote on it an inscription like the engraving of a signet: HOLINESS TO THE LORD. And they tied to it a blue cord, to fasten it above on the turban, as the LORD had commanded Moses. Thus all the work of the tabernacle of the tent of meeting was finished. (Ex. 39:30–32 NKJV)

Aaron was arrayed in beautiful priestly garments. Each piece that adorned him had specific significance, but notice the final finishing touch was a holy crown of pure gold inscribed with the words *HOLINESS TO THE LORD*. He was actually crowned with holiness. All the priestly garments and beautiful splendor were to declare Aaron God's own. Notice the plate was engraved like a signet; this is an important point. Signet rings had impressions within and without, and were capable of leaving impressions on things. When an edict or law was enacted, it was sealed with the imprint or impression of the signet ring, symbolizing who was actually behind the law.

Let's look at a natural example of this for a moment. In national and international beauty pageants, the winners are crowned, and a banner is draped on each of them to designate the country or state each represents. What would happen if, in the middle of the Miss Universe contest, Miss America decided she wanted to represent Japan? Would they let her? Of course not! She'd been chosen as an ambassador for America, not Japan; it is the American culture and people she is to represent and inspire. As priests, we are no different. We are to leave an impression on all those

> *We are to leave an impression on all those we meet that communicates whose we are and what kingdom we represent.*

we meet that communicates whose we are and what kingdom we represent. Peter continues his explanation of how we do this:

> Once you were not a people, but now you are the people of God; once you
> had not received mercy, but now you have received mercy. Dear friends, I
> urge you, as aliens and strangers in the world, to abstain from sinful desires,
> which war against your soul. Live such good lives among the pagans that,
> though they accuse you of doing wrong, they may see your good deeds and
> glorify God on the day he visits us. (1 Peter 2:10–12)

Once we were not God's, but now we are. Once we were under God's judgment, but now we've experienced His mercy. In other words, once we were in this world and under its sentence of judgment, but now we are not of this world, we are of God's kingdom. This makes us aliens and strangers on this earth where we were once citizens. As priests, we are God's representatives and ambassadors on this earth.

We bring forth sacrifices worthy of the king's mercy: our praises and our lives.

Holiness is about ownership; we no longer own our lives, He does. You may say, "I don't like the idea of someone owning me!" Whether you

> ∽ You were purchased at a
> great expense, and your praises
> are to declare His glory.

were aware of this or not, you were never truly free. You were born under the dominion of the kingdom of darkness and lived there as an enemy of God and a child destined for wrath. But a loving Prince has redeemed you. You were purchased at a great expense, and your praises are to declare His glory, along with the saints of heaven who sing the song of the Lamb.

> "You are worthy to take the scroll and to open its seals, because you were
> slain, and with *your blood* you *purchased men for God* from every tribe and language and people and nation. You have made them to be a kingdom and
> priests to serve our God, and they will reign on the earth." (Rev. 5:9–10,
> emphasis added)

Notice it says His blood purchased us for God, not for heaven. This Bridegroom redeemed His bride with His very life. But to understand the depths of this glorious romance, we must go back to a time period long ago and travel to a land far away where there are customs strange to us. Travel back with me to ancient Israel and observe the marriage rites and rituals. At this time, there was no dating; there were only brides and bridegrooms. Couples didn't temporarily try each other on for size and then go their separate ways. A great deal of commitment and good faith had already been established long before the final part of the marriage process even began.

> ⌒ *Couples didn't temporarily try each other on for size and then go their separate ways.*

When a son was of marrying age, he would ask his father to arrange a bride for him. The son might have had one in mind, but usually it was the father who would have been looking long before his son had thought about marriage. Together, they might discuss the merits of one daughter or another, but it was the father who ultimately chose the household and daughter they'd approach in order to acquire a bride for his son.

If their initial proposal was viewed favorably, the young man traveled to her home and met with her father and possibly any elder brothers to discuss the details and possibilities. The girl herself was not even involved in the initial negotiations. I am certain she waited in the wings, straining to see and hear what was going on in another room. Perhaps there were excited whispers as bit and pieces of the conversation drifted her way. "He is willing to give this for me!"

But her father would already have a price in mind. Girls were almost always exchanged for money because they were considered a financial loss to their families; they did not work the fields like a son, and therefore did not produce revenue for the household. If the father's expectations of a proposal were not met, the proposition of marriage was not even considered, and the negotiations were over. Although this may sound mercenary to us today, it was actually a form of protection for the girl. The father wanted an assurance his price would be met, but also that his daughter would be well taken care of. Back then girls were not given away by their fathers; they had to be first redeemed, then captured. Negotiations would go on for hours with questions, pledges of good faith, promises, and arguments as well.

When everything had been hashed out between the bride's father and the bridegroom, they would record it in a document, or marriage contract, which consisted of the designated bridal price, the pledges and promises of the groom, and the rights of the bride. This was a betrothal document, and when it was complete, a glass of wine would be poured, and the daughter, the potential bride, would be brought in.

All the hours of negotiation and the recording of every tedious detail would be wasted without her consent. She would be apprised of the offer on the table. Before her, the goblet of wine waited, representing the marriage covenant. She had two choices. She could refuse the wine poured before her, turn, and leave the room. If she did this, the marriage would not happen even though her father's terms had been agreed to. Or, she could say, "I do." If so, the cup was passed to the bridegroom who drank from it, then passed it to the bride. When she drank from the cup of the covenant, the contract was sealed.

The groom then gave the bride something of value to represent his sincerity to her and to their covenant. He stayed awhile with her so they could get to know one another better, but it was always under the watchful eye of her family. In our culture today, this gift is usually symbolized by an engagement ring. The two became legally betrothed, or bound in marriage, even though they did not yet live together.

The bride then underwent a baptism of water. This was an immersion ritual of cleansing and purification. It signified a separation, or a departure, from her former way of life and a cleansing in preparation for her new life with her husband. It was considered a type of spiritual rebirth for her. She was no longer alone; she was his.

After a while, the bridegroom would leave to return to his father's house. There, he would begin work on their home in preparation for their wedding. He would leave her with the statement, "I go to prepare a place for you; if I go, I will return again unto you." These are the same words of Jesus from John 14. Although it was hard to be separated, they understood they could never truly be completely together unless he first went to prepare a place.

> ⌒ He would leave her with the statement, "I go to prepare a place for you; if I go, I will return again unto you."

The bride was left with the covenant, the cup, the price paid in full, and a gift as her assurance her groom would return for her. She remained in her father's house and made herself ready. If she went out in public, she would wear a veil to signify she already belonged to another. Veiled women were called *set apart, sanctified, consecrated*, or *bought with a price*. (Sounds familiar, doesn't it?) Her life was tied by covenant to another. Her beauty was reserved for him. She was eager for his return and spent her time in readiness, preparing for their life together. She thought of him often as she gathered together her trousseau, especially as time passed, and she knew each day drew him nearer. She didn't want to miss her bridegroom's return; she wanted to be ready.

Let's stop here before we go any further and examine how these ancient marriage rituals reflect our relationship with Christ, for marriage is repeatedly referred to as a natural illustration of this.

> This is a profound mystery—but I am talking about Christ and the church. (Eph. 5:32)

Jesus left His heavenly home in pursuit of the bride His father had chosen for Him. He met the required purchase price to ransom her and make her his own. In this case, it cost Him all He had: His very life. He sealed this agreement when He drank of the cup at the Last Supper and then passed it to His disciples. He agreed to the negotiated price in the Garden of Gethsemane and paid it in full on the cross. Then, He presented His own blood as a sin offering and washed His bride with the water of the Word. This is the renewal process of mind, spirit, and soul that translates us from the kingdom of darkness to the kingdom of light.

Christ loved the church and gave himself up for her to make her holy, cleansing her by the washing with water through the word, and to present her to himself as a radiant church, without stain or wrinkle or any other blemish, but holy and blameless. (Eph. 5:25–27)

Notice Christ is the One who makes us holy. He redeems us to be His. We cannot redeem ourselves nor make ourselves holy. But we can make ourselves ready while He prepares a place for us.

For the wedding of the Lamb has come, and his bride has made herself ready. (Rev. 19:7)

The bride was responsible for maintaining an atmosphere and attitude of readiness. As Christ's bride, we are to assemble a wardrobe that will wait for our arrival there: "Fine linen, bright and clean, was given her to wear" (Rev. 19:8). Fine linen stands for the righteous acts of the saints.

Let's return now to our couple. The bride remains a lady in waiting, while the groom works diligently to prepare a bridal chamber for her by adding a room onto his father's house. This would take a lot of time and preparation, for at that time, there were no Home Depots where he could purchase his lumber. He would have to contract, or trade for lumber, or cut down trees, and prepare the place himself. All the while, he labored in delight, knowing his work would bring him closer to her. His father would keep a close watch on the son's progress and encourage and instruct him in the process. The father was also the one who would inspect the dwelling and tell the son when he believed it was ready for his bride. The bride's family as well might send delegates to make certain the bridegroom was making good on his word to his bride. They would report back to her, "It won't be long now. Be ready!"

Finally the work would pass the thorough inspection of the father, and he would turn to his son and tell him, "Go get your bride!" The bridegroom would gather his friends together, and with great rejoicing, they would go to get his bride. They would plan their departure so they could arrive at her place in the night. As they approached the city, they would sound a trumpet to alert the bride her lover was near. Of course, this sound would awaken every betrothed bride, and they would all wake, trembling with excitement. They would make ready their oil lamps by refreshing the oil in them and by trimming the wicks. (I think there would be teeth brushing and primping as well!) Then they would listen carefully for the announcement of the

> ⌒ The bride ran to her beloved with her lamp glowing and her handmaidens following. The groom swept her away to his father's house.

friends of the bridegroom. These friends would prepare a path for him outside of her parents' home and call to her, "Here's the bridegroom! Come out to meet him!" (Matt. 25:6).

Her father and brothers would go out to check and be certain this was the right guy calling to their daughter. They certainly didn't want to send her off with the wrong bridegroom! After confirming his identity, they would turn their backs on her departure. It almost seemed like an abduction or a kidnapping. The bride ran to her beloved with her lamp glowing and her handmaidens following. The groom swept her away, and they returned immediately to his father's house, where the two entered the bridal chamber. For the next seven days, they would enjoy their love behind a sealed door.

The bridegroom's friends would sit outside the door and wait for the moment of joy when the marriage was in fact consummated. When they heard his voice, they announced his joy to the others present, and the celebration was under way. The bed sheet would be passed out through a window. This was given to her father as proof of his daughter's virtue in case any question of it was raised in the future. The shed blood of her hymen represented the final sealing of the covenant. After the seven days together, she would remove the veil, come out with the bridegroom, and the marriage banquet would begin. Wine and food would flow freely in celebration of their joy. Blessings would be pronounced over them, and gifts would be given.

This is a glorious and romantic reflection of Jesus and His bride. He has truly gone to prepare a place for us. He comes quickly, and His reward is with Him. We must ready ourselves for His return.

"Therefore keep watch, because you do not know the day or the hour." (Matt. 25:13)

⌒ Dear Heavenly Father,

Reveal by Your spirit any areas that I have yet to separate unto You. I want to be holy, to be completely Yours. Teach me the ways of a bride so my heart might rejoice in a constant state of readiness. May my lamp always be ready and filled with oil. Open the eyes of my heart so I might see clearly this season. I want to walk as a faithful bride, not as a wicked servant who whispers in her heart, My Lord delays His coming. I want the separation and consecration of my life to leave an impression on others. May they know I am Yours and You are mine. Veil me by Your Spirit until I can rejoice and see You face to face.

Love,

Your Daughter

12 The Power of Purity

*C*an the young be strong and free? Paul certainly thought so:

> Don't let anyone look down on you because you are young, but set an
> example for the believers in speech, in life, in love, in faith and in purity. (1
> Tim. 4:12)

This verse almost seems to state a contradiction. Paul is charging a *young* man to be an example for believers? Today we rarely think of the young and single as shining examples of faith and purity. Yet Paul is challenging Timothy to hold his head high and not allow his youth to be a factor for intimidation. If a young person is charged to be an example in speech, life, love, faith, and purity, how much more should those of us who are mature in our years live holy lives?

You have the grace of God, His very empowerment, to walk in this exhortation. You *can*, regardless of age, live a life that exemplifies purity to those watching you.

> ⁓ *You can live a life that exemplifies purity to those watching you.*

At first glance, purity may seem the same as holiness, but it is not. Remember, holiness means to be set apart, whereas purity is how you conduct yourself because you're consecrated. Purity is the by-product of holiness. In this chapter, we're going to address some issues often skirted in religious circles but celebrated openly in secular arenas. I will counsel you by the wisdom and warnings found in the Word of God, as well as from my years of experience in the ministry. I want to help you build a foundation that cannot be shaken, so hang on tight: we'll be delving into a lot of Scriptures.

God wants to be our life source. If you are truly brave, invite the Holy Spirit to examine your heart and motives by the light of God's piercing and penetrating Word. This is not for the faint of heart.

> For the word of God is living and active. Sharper than any double-edged sword, it penetrates even to dividing soul and spirit, joints and marrow; it judges the thoughts and attitudes of the heart. Nothing in all creation is hidden from God's sight. Everything is uncovered and laid bare before the eyes of him to whom we must give account. (Heb. 4:12–13)

God's Word is not merely letters on paper . . . it's alive. Believe and draw near, for it longs to dance in your heart and whisper to you in the night. It is so sharp it can separate the soul from the spirit, and in the process, reveal our hidden thoughts and attitudes.

Remember nothing (no thing) is hidden from God. He sees it all, but we do not. Often our very own hearts deceive us, but if we ask for truth, God will share His discernment with us

> ⌐ God's Word is not merely letters on paper . . . it's alive. Believe and draw near, for it longs to dance in your heart and whisper to you in the night.

through His Word. I don't want the counsel of man . . . I want the wisdom and insight of God. The counsel of man is always influenced by the culture and standards of this age. It is foolishness that readjusts itself every decade or so, reflecting the moral temperature of society. But God's Word stands forever, and it is the standard to which we will give an account.

You will be confronted with truths in this chapter that may initially seem impossible or unrealistic . . . but they are not. It is a lie to believe He is incapable of keeping His promises, and He has promised to keep us from falling and to present us blameless before the throne. We will know truth, and it will make us free. First, we are going to visit some pointed Scriptures, then we're going to answer some questions in light of the truth. We want to guard from moving toward rules because God's call to holiness is about being His.

> But among you there must not be *even a hint* of sexual immorality, or of any kind of impurity, or of greed, because these are improper for God's holy people. (Eph. 5:3, emphasis added)

How strong is this verse? We are not even allowed a *hint* of sexual immorality, impurity, or greed! Why? What's so bad about just a little hint, if I'm not actually doing anything major? Well, what is the purpose of a hint, if not to give clues that suggest more exists than what's immediately seen? This type of behavior (or even the hint of it) is not acceptable for those who are His. According to the *Microsoft Word Dictionary*, the word *improper* is defined as "rude, shocking, indecent, inappropriate, offensive," and lastly "not the done thing!"

This type of behavior sends a mixed message to those around us that is confusing. For example, wearing a low-cut, cleavage-revealing top is called *suggestive*. What does it suggest? That there is more than what you now see, and I may let you look closer since I'm already willing to give you this much of a peek. (We'll discuss this further later.) As God's, we are marked for Him, and are to honor Him in all we say and do. This means both the words we speak and our conduct should bear His image. We are more than just forgiven; we are holy unto Him. We are to be light where we were once darkness. Let's continue in this Scripture in Ephesians:

> Nor should there be obscenity, foolish talk or coarse joking, which are out of place, but rather thanksgiving. (Eph. 5:4)

Add to the list of improper behavior, no obscene, foolish, or coarse talk. I guess they had dirty jokes back then as well, for there is, after all, nothing new under the sun (Eccl. 1:9). Too often, we do not realize the power of our own words to bless or defile others. Let's break each of those categories down so there is no question as to their meaning:

- **Obscenity** is speech that is impure or lewd in expression or representation by words, gesture, or pictures.

- **Foolish** talk is wicked, sinful speech, without regard to divine law, God's glory, or one's eternal happiness. (Yikes!)

- **Coarse** talk is gross, impure, rude, rough, unrefined, or mean speech.

Instead of punctuating our conversation with these types of speech, we are to be fluent in thanksgiving. We are to maintain an attitude of thankfulness for the favors and mercy God has already extended to us. This alone should be enough to keep some of us talking for quite a while. We are not to be crude, rude whiners and com-

> ⌒ *Let no one deceive you with empty words. Empty words are void of life.*

plainers. We are to act like God, blessing and releasing life through our conversations, living in the Spirit with a thankful heart. Paul continues:

For of this you can be sure: No immoral, impure or greedy person—such a man who is an idolater—has any inheritance in the kingdom of Christ and of God. Let no one deceive you with empty words, for because of such things God's wrath comes on those who are disobedient. Therefore do not be partners with them. (Eph. 5:5–7)

In case we didn't get it the first time, He is making sure we clearly understand the context of this warning and directive, *Let no one deceive you with empty words.* Empty words are void of life. They have no real power in them to bring about change in you, but they do have the power to deceive you. Remember, God's Word is sharp and alive and brings us to repentance. Empty words are dull and dead and lull us into a sleep of complacency, deceiving those who do not use the sword of the Word of

God to rightly divide truth from error. No matter how nice empty words may sound, ultimately they will not lead you to life. Some of these examples of empty words you may have heard:

"It's okay . . . we're all in the growth process."
"God knows your heart."
"No one's perfect."
"Everyone else is doing it."
"You're doing better than most."

These are words of compromise, and even though they may be true, they are not living words of truth. Truth inspires us to change, to leave behind our ways and strive to rise higher to God's perspective. His way of thinking is totally different than the way we process things. Empty words only encourage us to stay the same by offering excuses for our behavior in relation to our present cultural standards. But we are no longer in relationship with our culture; we are in relationship with God.

Don't you know that friendship with the world is hatred toward God? (James 4:4)

Our counsel cannot be the wit and wisdom of this present world, but the Word of God. Christians are called to encourage one another. This means we bring courage to each other by speaking the promises of God. To answer these empty words, we have God's counsel:

It's okay . . . we're all in the growth process. Are we in process? Yes! But our destination is not the process; it is transformation, and we are promised that He who began a good work will carry it out until completion (Phil. 1:6).

God knows your heart. Out of the overflow of your heart, your mouth will speak. The good man brings good things out of the good stored up in him, and the evil man brings evil things out of the evil stored up in him (Matt. 12:34–35). What you say reveals your heart.

No one's perfect. Be perfect, therefore, as your heavenly Father is perfect (Matt. 5:48). Ouch! Even though the righteous man falls seven times, he still gets up (Prov. 24:16).

Everyone else is doing it. I tell you this, and insist on it in the Lord, that you must no longer live as the Gentiles do, in the futility of their thinking (Eph. 4:17–18).

You're doing better than most. We should not dare to classify or compare ourselves with some who commend themselves. When they measure themselves by themselves and compare themselves with themselves, they are not wise (2 Cor. 10:12–13). Who wants to be stupid when we can be wise? Stop looking at others, and look at the perfect law of liberty!

We have to settle this: God and His Word are truth, and the counsel of man is a lie. The Word of the Lord is not to be watered down until it blends seamlessly with the counsel of man or the insights of New Age gurus. The Word of God has always stood alone, and it alone has endured the test of time. It has been handed down to us as a glorious treasury of wisdom and guidance. Let us therefore be faithful witnesses of truth, and press and urge each other onward toward the mark.

A decade ago John and I visited Israel, I still remember what our Arab tour guide told us about the Romans. He claimed they were benevolent conquerors, and even allowed the Jewish people to maintain their own *religious beliefs*; they just wanted them to take on the Roman *culture*. They wanted them to look, live, and act like Romans. I am not certain the invasion tactics have changed much since then.

> ⟋ *The Word of the Lord is not to be watered down until it blends seamlessly with the counsel of man or the insights of New Age gurus.*

We hear the counsel of this present age calling, "You may have your religion, but please enjoy this world too! Relax. Blend in! Why struggle against the powers of this age? You can believe whatever you want . . . just act like us!" But of course, this won't work for us. God has never called us to blend in. Let's revisit the book of James:

> You adulterous people, don't you know that friendship with the world is hatred toward God? Anyone who chooses to be a friend of the world becomes an enemy of God. (James 4:4)

When we walk with a foot in both worlds, we experience struggles, because our hearts are divided. David and the prophet Ezekiel both understood the need for an undivided heart:

> Teach me your way, O LORD, and I will walk in your truth; *give me an undivided heart,* that I may fear your name. (Ps. 86:11, emphasis added)

> *I will give them an undivided heart* and put a new spirit in them; I will remove from them their heart of stone and give them a heart of flesh. Then they will follow my decrees and be careful to keep my laws. They will be my people, and I will be their God. (Ezek. 11:18–20, emphasis added)

I believe you have this book in your hand because you desire to serve God with a whole and undivided heart. This means your body will follow the direction set by your heart. Never before has the call to purity been more urgent, pressing, or difficult.

> And do this, understanding the present time. The hour has come for you to wake up from your slumber, because our salvation is nearer now than when we first believed. The night is nearly over; the day is almost here. (Rom. 13:11–12)

There is an urgent cry in the spirit for us to awaken to righteousness. How do we do this? We use the sword of the spirit, the Word of God, to sever every entanglement tethering our hearts to this fallen world. He wants there to be no struggle for our affections. He invites us to place our hearts in the safety of His care and then wage war on the enemies of our souls.

> ⌐ *There is an urgent cry in the spirit for us to awaken to righteousness.*

Put to death, therefore, whatever belongs to your earthly nature: sexual immorality, impurity, lust, evil desires and greed, which is idolatry. Because of these, the wrath of God is coming. (Col. 3:5–6)

There it is again: the promise of God's wrath on sexual immorality, impurity, and greed. God admonishes us to sever our ties with objects of His wrath. If we are to faithfully wield the sword, we must realize and submit to the power of it. God's Word has the power to disengage us from the power of sin.

I am operating on the assumption that if you picked up this book, you are in fact looking for answers to some questions. I am going to do my best to answer you straight. Of course, you are free to disagree with my views, for they are certainly not moderate or middle of the road, but I do believe they are biblically sound. In this chapter, we are going to address purity in the area of word and deed. In the next chapter, we'll speak of it in light of our appearances and apparel.

Remember some of the questions we raised in Chapter 1? Let's begin with "How far is too far?" You probably remember my answer. You can go as far with your boyfriends as you are comfortable going in front of your fathers. This was my attempt to push this issue out of your box of rules and into a realm of relationships. Let's go deeper with this question . . . when does sexual involvement outside of marriage actually become sin?

Is it with the first passionate kiss; is it the touching of breasts over clothing? Or do we break the sin barrier when shirts are lifted and articles of underclothing are removed? Maybe everything above the waist is permissible, but once the boundary of the waistline is crossed, then you're in big trouble. Or is touching over clothing below the waist all right, but once this barrier of cloth is removed then you're trespassing on dangerous ground? Once these physical boundaries are violated and everything private is exposed to the sight of the eye and the touch of the hand, are we still pure because there has been no sexual penetration? Or is it all right to add in oral stimulation because, after all, it is not actually sexual intercourse? Having gone this far, isn't it unkind not to provide some form of sexual release for all the buildup? This would involve moving from mere oral stimulation to oral sex. And how amazing this can all happen without even losing your actual physical virginity! Though a couple engaged in this type of sexual behavior may physiologically and technically still be virgins . . . is either of them pure?

> ⌒ *Sin does not begin in the physical realm; it begins in the form of desire.*

When you begin down this path, every action brings with it its own set of reasoning and arguments to convince you to continue to move forward in your desire and actions. You feel as though a floodgate has been opened, and now you must strain against a powerful flow stronger than both of you. It is an awesome, ageless, and passionate torrent that has been raging since the beginning of time.

Let's return to our original question . . . At what point did the actions become sin? Is it with kissing, touching, disrobing, or with sexual release? Surprisingly enough, it does not begin with any one of these. Sin does not begin in the physical realm; it begins in the form of desire. This is why Jesus could say those who looked at women with lust were guilty of adultery.

> But each one is tempted when, by his own evil desire, he is dragged away and enticed. Then, after desire has conceived, it gives birth to sin; and sin, when it is full-grown, gives birth to death. (James 1:14–15)

Look at this: He is "dragged away and enticed"! Who does this? Is it when a boy drags away a girl and entices her, or when a woman seduces a man? No! *Our own desires* will pull us out of the light of truth, isolate us from wisdom, and all the while demand gratification. If indulged, desire becomes pregnant with sin. Pregnancy is when something is living and growing inside of us, even though it has yet to come forth into the light. Its presence is there, growing stronger with each passing day, until eventually what is within can no longer be withheld, and it comes forth out of the dark womb into the light.

Let's turn bravely to another prominent question often skirted in Christian circles. What about masturbation? Is it all right since it is not specifically forbidden in the Bible?

Well, even though masturbation may not be mentioned by name in Scripture, I do believe the Bible addresses this. This is something we can judge by its fruit. Masturbation can be addictive in nature, and, it definitely feeds and strengthens the effect of desire. It may begin with just a physical release or need, but it rarely stays there. As time passes, it intertwines itself with fantasy and often pornography. These may be past or present images recalled from movies, videos, photos, or even past sexual activity. It schools its participants in self-gratification and is the very opposite of intimacy, for its focus is only on one's self. We have been commanded to put to death what belonged to our earthly nature and follow the nature of the Cross, which is a daily walk of self-denial.

Having lost all sensitivity, they have given themselves over to sensuality so as to indulge in every kind of impurity, with a continual lust for more. (Eph. 4:19)

The words *given themselves over* speak of surrender, a yielding of our wills to the charge or wishes of another. Whenever we yield to sensuality, it is like throwing yet another log on the bonfire of lust, and the fading flame threatens to rage out of control. At first, we dull the senses, and then we eventually lose all sensitivity to the things of the Spirit. We become driven by the whims of sensuality, or our sensory realm, rather than be led by the Holy Spirit. Each act of indulgence reinforces lust and strengthens the stronghold, or fortress, of the habit; this protects and

> ⌒ *Whenever we yield to sensuality, it is like throwing yet another log on the bonfire of lust.*

prolongs its life and strengthens its hold. In nineteen years of ministry, I have never spoken with a sex addict or a couple wrestling with sexual dysfunction with whom masturbation was not a major issue, even after they were married.

I have heard masturbation endorsed with the argument that to the pure in heart, all things are pure. But we cannot call "pure" what leads to impurity, no matter how pure our own hearts may be. Nor can we put under the category of lawful what God's counsel would contradict as otherwise. I believe masturbation is a violation of the fruit of the spirit *self-control* (Gal. 5:23; 2 Peter 1:6), and purity of thought (Phil. 4:8).

> That each of you should learn to control his own body in a way that is holy and honorable. (1 Thess. 4:4)

In contrast, the fruit of delayed gratification produces patience, endurance, and self-control. These in turn develop physical, emotional, and spiritual longing. If this longing is allowed to have its work in us, it will create a passion to share this place of longing with another. When we refuse to fill it for ourselves, we capture the essence of longing and intimacy, because intimacy is something shared, not something spent alone.

Self-gratification and masturbation, if indulged, eventually feed selfishness. This in turn fosters lust, and you will begin to have the idea others exist solely to satiate your desires.

It has long been assumed all boys masturbate. Much of this thinking was tied to the pornography they were often exposed to. But now girls have joined their privileged ranks with the blanket assumption that girls behave this way as well. Women begin to think there is something wrong with them if they are not involved in

> ⌒ *The fruit of delayed gratification produces patience, endurance, and self-control. These in turn develop physical, emotional, and spiritual longing.*

this form of sexual release. Many women's magazines not only encourage masturbation, but often instruct their readers in it. Where are we heading with all this? We have lost so much beauty. Of course, if we continue down this road, some women will conclude they only need men if they want to become pregnant.

As a closing comment, I do not believe masturbation fosters purity, and therefore, it is not expedient to the health of our desire to walk pure before a holy God. It attempts to meet valid human needs in an invalid way that leads down a path to selfishness. Taking up the cross is about denying your flesh, not indulging it. If you are

> *Taking up the cross is about denying your flesh, not indulging it.*

single, pour your passion into your relationship with God or into helping others. If you are married, wives are charged to have chaste behavior even in their marriages. Purity is still an issue in marriage. We are to guard and keep our marriage beds pure.

> Marriage should be honored by all, and the marriage bed kept pure, for God will judge the adulterer and all the sexually immoral. (Heb. 13:4)

This is not a blanket Scripture to say anything goes in the marriage bed. It says it is to be honored, kept free from adultery and sexual immorality. This would include pornography and sexual fantasies of others. One precious woman confessed to me she did not enjoy sex with her husband unless she was fantasizing it was taking place back before they were married. They had been involved in premarital sex, and nearly twenty years later, she still returns to the bed of sin to gather her inspiration. We prayed, and she renounced that involvement as sin and asked God to make their marriage bed pure and passionate.

Another big question that comes up is the issue of oral sex. Of course, it would be sin if it occurred outside of marriage, but what about in the marriage? Is oral sex okay? I know others will disagree with me, but I personally do not believe a woman's throat was ever meant for the seed of a man. Sexual intercourse is when two become one, with the ability to produce life from their union. It is unique to the relationship between a man and a woman. Oral sex is not. It can happen in homosexual relations, but of course, true sexual intercourse cannot. Adam knew his wife. He entered her womb and planted his seed there.

As far as the issue of homosexuality, I believe God created men as men and women as women, in other words, heterosexuals. He did not then decide to make a second race of people and call them homosexuals. There is no such thing. There are only males and females struggling with homosexual desires, but they are not a new breed or race of people. It is a lie to allow them to think they have no choice. God is very strong in His position on homosexual behavior:

> If a man lies with a man as one lies with a woman, both of them have done what is detestable. They must be put to death; their blood will be on their own heads. (Lev. 20:13)

This Scripture may seem rather strong, but don't forget that under the law God prescribed the death penalty for adulterers as well as homosexuals. It is a purity issue. Homosexuality and adultery violate the Genesis plan of one man and one woman becoming one before God.

> ⌒ Homosexuality and adultery violate the Genesis plan of one man and one woman becoming one before God.

There are a number of accounts of homosexuality in the Old Testament, and it is never embraced as an alternative lifestyle. Not until Paul speaks of the last days do we see the shift to that way of thinking.

> Because of this, God gave them over to shameful lusts. Even their women exchanged natural relations for unnatural ones. In the same way the men also abandoned natural relations with women and were inflamed with lust for one another. Men committed indecent acts with other men, and received in themselves the due penalty for their perversion. (Rom. 1:26–27)

Unnatural desires and indecent acts are the result of a culture that exchanges the truth of God for a lie of man. If God calls something unnatural, shameful, and indecent, it was never in His original plan. God is not confused on this issue; we are. He longs to set free those who are bound to lust, whether it is from fornication, pornography, adultery, or homosexuality, or inordinate affections. I am not saying escaping the bondage of homosexual desires is easy, but it is possible.

Pornographic images are, of course, a violation of purity. When you look at pornographic images, regardless of the medium, you are sharing in the shame of another. You become party to it, and it will have a hold on you like no other images you will encounter. You may have to strain to recall any other images you saw in a movie, but you will easily remember the ones containing sexual nudity. They are filed in the front of your mind, just hoping you will pull them out. They are tenacious because it is a shared sin. Remember when Noah's two sons refused to look at their father's nakedness and backed into the tent with a garment to cover him? This is a big deal. You were never meant to look at the shame of others.

> *You were never meant to look at the shame of others.*

I will set before my eyes no vile thing. (Ps. 101:3)

And again:

Will you defile yourselves the way your fathers did and lust after their vile images? (Ezek. 20:30)

Pornography will torment your conscience and war against your marriage bed. If you've participated in it, repent, and then ask God to help you tear down those images through prayer, time in His presence, the Word, and praising Him.

We are not called to shame, but to purity. Because we have wanted to avoid the feelings of shame at all costs, we have embraced the shameful. We

> ⌒ *We must choose whose words we will listen to, the words of our Savior or the words of the tempter who seeks our life.*

have compromised rather than pressed in. I am passionate to see the power of purity reign in the life of every woman, whether she is single or married, young or old. Hear the passion and commission of Paul and make it your own:

> I am jealous for you with a godly jealousy. I promised you to one husband, to Christ, so that I might present you as a pure virgin to him. But I am afraid that just as Eve was deceived by the serpent's cunning, your minds may somehow be led astray from your sincere and pure devotion to Christ. (2 Cor. 11:2–3)

Sin always seems to come back to the serpent's attempt to lead us astray from our pure devotion to Christ. We must choose whose words we will listen to: the words of our Savior or the words of the tempter who seeks our life. It is the Word of God, not the word of a preacher, counselor, or teacher, that is the ultimate authority. If you ask God, He will take the sword of the Spirit and cut away every falsehood from your life.

Even with all of these outward modifications, we must return to the root issue; purity of thought produces purity of actions, appearance, and conversations. No matter how much we struggle, if enough pressure is applied to us in any given situation, we will eventually falter in any battle, if we have not already won the war inwardly. I have tried to give you what I believe is in accordance with the whole counsel of God's Word. I know some of this teaching may seem to be hard truths, so I want to close with some additional Scriptures for your study. May you never preach the counsel and compromise of men and call it the wisdom of God.

> Do you not know that your bodies are members of Christ himself? Shall I then take the members of Christ and unite them with a prostitute? Never! Do you not know that he who unites himself with a prostitute is one with her in body? For it is said, "The two will become one flesh." But he who unites himself with the Lord is one with him in spirit. Flee from sexual

immorality. All other sins a man commits are outside his body, but he who sins sexually sins against his own body. Do you not know that your body is a temple of the Holy Spirit, who is in you, whom you have received from God? You are not your own; you were bought at a price. Therefore honor God with your body. (1 Cor. 6:15–20)

The acts of the sinful nature are obvious: sexual immorality, impurity and debauchery . . . I warn you, as I did before, that those who live like this will not inherit the kingdom of God. (Gal. 5:19–21)

It is God's will that you should be sanctified: that you should avoid sexual immorality; that each of you should learn to control his own body in a way that is holy and honorable, not in passionate lust like the heathen, who do not know God. (1 Thess. 4:3–5)

> ⌒ *Dear Heavenly Father,*
>
> *I want to know You in every area of my life. You are the very essence of truth, light, love, purity, and holiness. I am Yours, and I commit to tremble at Your Word. I will allow it honor, preeminence, and authority in my everyday life. I invite its sword into every area and ask You to act as the Great Physician, removing the precious from the vile. With the skill of a master surgeon, remove every entanglement in my heart and every defilement in my sexuality so I may be wholly Yours, set apart for Your pleasure and purpose. I embrace Your Word of truth and turn aside from the standard of this world. In Jesus' name. Amen.*
>
> *Love,*
> *Your Daughter*

13 *Dressed to Kill*

$\mathcal{W}$e are always communicating, whether we intend to or not. Our messages will go out through one of three channels: *what we say* (our words and tone), *what we do* (our manners and actions), and *what we look like* (our visual appearances or presentations). We discussed our conversation and our actions in the last chapter, but the impact of our appearances is a truth of equal weight that cannot be neglected. It is a major issue because people are often more influenced by what they see than by what they hear. This is truer for men than women because men are so much more sight-oriented and visually wired.

When we understand this, we can use this power to our advantage and communicate our intentions effectively. We don't want to send out mixed messages and sabotage what we really wanted to say. I am certain that you've heard one form or another of the old adage, *You never get a second chance to make a good first impression.* Well, it may be old, but it was certainly never truer. In our culture image is everything, visual images have become very explicit and extreme, and self-expression has never been so wide in its range. For example, hair color can be anything from green to purple. Lips are no longer limited to the natural shades of pink, rose, or red . . . now black is a fashion option. In our wardrobes any length or style goes. There have never been so many options for expression, but what exactly are we saying? Are we any more efficient with all this freedom of expression?

For example, if you want a guy to appreciate you for your mind, don't overwhelm him with your cleavage and navel. Your point will be lost. If you confuse your signals or mix your messages, something is bound to be lost in the interpretation. Guys will have a hard time looking beyond your most obvious attributes to notice your amazing, unseen IQ.

> ⌒ *If you want a guy to appreciate you for your mind, don't overwhelm him with your cleavage and navel.*

How you dress and present yourself not only sends an obvious and immediate message to others, but it may imply more than you really intended to make known. It may betray what you really think of yourself. Or what you trust in. Or where you think your power comes from. Or, of course, *to whom you belong.*

Think about that one for a moment. My boys talk about the different cliques in their school, which are strongly separated by dress style. Goths dress in gothic clothes and preps dress in preppy clothes. When we're shopping I'll ask my sons, "What about this shirt?" and I'll hear, "No, that's a skater brand." How was I to know? The kids sure have the system down; if they are not skaters, they will not pose as one by what they wear. Another example we can relate to is the terms *white-collar* and *blue-collar*. One is used to describe professional office careers; the other describes those in the working class. These terms indicate certain dress styles, including their accompanying signals and prejudices.

What are you presently communicating? What messages are you sending? Are they an accurate reflection of who you are, or are you just posing? These are very important questions, and you need to take a moment to honestly answer them. Your outward dress and appearance may accurately reflect who you are. You may say, "I am a professional, and my dress is appropriate for my profession." Or you might be a student and feel you are part of the "preps," which your style of dress reflects well. But let's dig a little deeper.

How are you affecting others by your manner of clothing? Are you encouraging males to have godly thought patterns or desires? Do people see you or only what you are wearing? When others look at you, what do they see?

You may be pulling from your Scripture memory bank and arguing that appearance shouldn't matter, because God looks at the heart, and we shouldn't judge by appearance. Well, thank heavens He looks at our hearts, but we do still live on the earth, and everyone here looks at the exterior, because only God sees the interior.

Man looks at the outward appearance, but the LORD looks at the heart. (1 Sam. 16:7)

This verse states the fact: We are moved by what we see. We're exhorted to be careful of confusing others by the way we package ourselves. We have been warned vanity is a fleeting hope, and it is therefore foolish to trust in our looks.

Let's go back to the question we posed in Chapter 1: Is it okay to dress seductively? How much skin should you show at any one time? I want to approach this a little deeper with you. The way we attract a man is the way he'll expect to be maintained. For example, a seductive outfit visually promises sex. The way we dress is not limited to just a form of self-expression, a way to communicate our personal or professional value. It is bigger than any of these. Let's raise the stakes a little . . . as children of God, we must understand that everything in our lives is ultimately about honoring our Father.

> ⌒ It is always easier to deal in extremes, whether they are legalistic or loose. I am going to challenge you to think a little more responsibly.

Please don't shut down or go religious on me and imagine I'm advocating the shapeless tent of veils. . . I'm not. I do believe we can be fashionable and attractive without being molded into a worldly image. But to do this requires some personal finesse, because it is always easier to deal in extremes, whether they are legalistic or loose. I am going to challenge you to think a little more responsibly about what you choose to wear. Because the lines are being blurred daily, it sometimes appears that Christians are no longer a counterculture but a copycat subculture.

It so happened that while writing this book I caught a daytime TV talk show that was highlighting the desperation of mothers whose daughters were in total rebellion. It seems these girls refused to wear a decent amount of clothing when they went out in public. They loved the attention it drew for them. One wore only a bathing suit top and a mini sarong while she strutted her stuff. Another wore an orange wig, tight halter, and supershort shorts over her large body. These girls were only fourteen and fifteen, and both boasted of their involvement with sex, drugs, and alcohol.

They looked like used-up hookers. Gone was any freshness or innocence of youth. Their mothers wept as though their girls were dead, so complete was their transformation from children to sluts. Through tears the mothers spoke of the past beauty of their daughters and the pain of shame their daughters' behavior had brought upon their families. They shared how they feared they would one day wake to find them dead in some alley. All the while, both girls laughed and cursed at their mothers and at anyone in the audience who challenged them. Their language was so foul that almost every other word out of their mouths was censored. I began to weep over their deception and the horrible frustration of their helpless, hopeless mothers.

These mothers had to be at the end of their ropes to hope that putting their exhibitionist daughters on national television would bring them to their senses. Why were these mothers so powerless? How did it get this far? And where in the world were these girls' fathers?

There was nothing I'd call feminine about these girls. It was a stretch to even imagine anyone classifying them as "sexy"; I would have categorized their appearance as "raunchy." I was embarrassed for them. I know that in their disillusionment they thought they looked to be the equal of some pop singers, but they did not. I felt violated as a woman just looking at them. They had no shame or beauty because there was no remnant of modesty or wisdom left in them. There was only total defiance, thrown in the faces of their weeping mothers.

It was obvious that they felt their wardrobes (or lack thereof) had given them power. They mistakenly equated their ability to inspire lust with personal empowerment. They walked down the street and imagined that the grasping men actually wanted them. If they had been a little smarter, they would have realized that none of these men really wanted them; they just wanted to relieve themselves of sexual tension. But these little girls had confused being conquered with power. It's not like these men were asking them to share their lives. They only wanted to violate them and then toss them aside, but these foolish girls just didn't get it.

> ⌐ *They mistakenly equated their ability to inspire lust with personal empowerment.*

Their dress represents a deeper power struggle in their lives. In the past when one country warred against another, the victors would indulge themselves in the privileged frenzy of taking spoils. This final blow was the most humiliating revenge and crueler than any offense unleashed on the battlefield. They would ravage the safety and honor of the home and family by burning houses and raping women. This was considered to be the utter degradation of their defeated enemy. There is certainly no historical record of the women enjoying this plunder. They ran in terror and hid from these warring men.

But the confused girls I saw on the talk show would never have recognized this as rape and violation, or even realized that the real issue wasn't sexual but a question of honor. They would have been out there in the streets, welcoming them and thinking they were getting a prize, that their beauty was what had drawn these predators to them.

> ⌐ *Their dress represents a deeper power struggle in their lives.*

They don't realize that with each sexual encounter they are degraded a bit more. Their image of beauty and womanhood is reduced quickly to the attraction of a five-dollar hooker, mere sexual release.

Let's visit the image of seduction that so many are trying to copy, the one that promises them power. What is this image telling us? There are so many messengers in this camp we can listen to. They range from teens to surgically enhanced baby boomers. These images stare disdainfully at us from magazine covers in every airport, convenience store, or grocery store. With their haughty heads lifted high above exaggerated breasts, they say, "I am powerful! Listen to my wisdom." *Cosmo, Allure, In Style,* or almost any other woman's magazine promises you the secrets to thin thighs and mind-blowing sex. They will make you the best prostitute you can possibly be.

Once when passing by the unavoidable display of magazines in the checkout line, my nine-year-old son moved a little closer to me and whispered, "Mommy, I think that woman looks like she wants to eat me!" I guess he found her wantonness a little frightening. I actually think quite a few men feel the same way, even if they are not as aware of that feeling as my innocent son.

The blatant, aggressive, in-your-face type of seductive appearance can threaten a man's machismo by connecting first with his basest level of arousal. He may sense a potential conquest in the air, and his testosterone level rises to meet the challenge of this opponent. He must then recover his own power by taking her down. It is as though men are constantly being taunted by sexually aggressive women, on everything from magazine covers to billboards, not to mention the gyrating divas of music videos, all daring in unison, *You want a piece of me? You can look at me, but I am always going to be just out of your reach.* These images remain in their minds, but since they can't get their hands on the women in print or on television, they go for the posers.

If men were to believe every women's magazine cover and pornographic publication, they would think all women really do want sex, even if they say no. They would think that we don't really mean what we say; it's only part of some sexual fantasy game. Even in the movies, the tie between sex and power is beginning to loom larger than the old-fashioned notion of sex and love. There is even a weaving of sex and death. You are never certain: Do they want to have sex with each other or kill one another?

Wake up! Don't listen to these lies! Where is the power they promised you? It was fleeting. You are not winning; you are being conquered. You are being stripped naked and raped. Where is your honor? Where is your strength? Where is your dignity? It has fled from you.

> *Wake up! Don't listen to these lies! Where is the power they promised you?*

When I look at these women I see folly. They may look beautiful on the outside, but I doubt the depth of true beauty within them. True beauty inspires the desire to protect or preserve it. True feminine beauty graces both the young and the old with its loveliness. These images that are being paraded before us would do little to flatter anyone except the youth who will to dare to bare. There is no softness, no safety, and no promise of comfort from the storms of life to be found in the arms of these seductresses. Perhaps you imagine I am just jealous because I am older, but I am not. I do understand the initial attraction to this image and her promise of power. I have been there and done that, and it left me empty and hungry for someone who would truly love and protect me. I got tired of being a warrior or a challenge, and instead, I longed to be adored.

As we mentioned earlier, if a woman does not connect in her childhood and youth with her father in a healthy manner, it will have an adverse effect on her response to men. (That is, unless she is intercepted by a prince, as I was.) Fathers should adore their daughters and treat them as though they were a precious treasure. I lost my eye at five and with it any hope of ever feeling pretty and feminine. I was called "one-eye" and "Cyclops" at school, and neither name made me feel desirable. After the loss of my eye, my father withdrew from me as well, so I learned to be tough to survive. When my father did connect with me at all, it was through his pride in my tough skin. His pet names for me were "tiger" and "little scrapper." Somehow dresses and feminine things didn't fit with these images. So in order to be safe, I determined never to be a sissy or a girly girl.

Then one Saturday in junior high while watching a movie, I found the image of a woman I identified with. She was not dressed in pink, and there was nothing frilly or lacy about her. Her life was an exciting adventure.

She was one of the elite Bond girls (as in James). I was definitely more comfortable with the image of these seductive chicks wearing hot pants, packing guns, and running with the boys. They held their own with the men, and no one dared push them around. They weren't going to wait for some man to protect them . . . they'd do it themselves.

> ⌒ *I was definitely more comfortable with the image of these seductive chicks wearing hot pants, packing guns, and running with the boys.*

I had seen this type of woman in a magazine before. It was one a friend and I had found hidden in her father's drawers. It was called *Playboy*. I reasoned these were the kind of women all men secretly wanted, which is why they brought them into their homes. Let me give you a side warning here, Mom and Dad, don't ever think you can actually hide something in your house—you can't. This type of material has a voice that calls to your children until they find it.

Back to my story: I was thirteen at the time of the movie moment and had already determined men couldn't be trusted. After all, my father had divorced himself from us, and I assumed all men eventually leave. This prejudice caused me to make a very grave mistake that affected my life determination at this young age. But the culture around me continued to reaffirm the attractiveness of my choice, with the popularity of the TV show *Charlie's Angels* when I was in high school.

There was one incident at an afternoon pep rally in my high school, when a group of us was doing a skit to the song "California Girls." Now mind you, I was terrified of anything that put me up in front of more than two people, but somehow I'd gotten involved with this skit, and my line was "and the northern girls with the way they kiss, they keep their boyfriends warm at night." I didn't see how I could possibly pull it off without fainting. But that all changed the night before the skit when I tried on my costume: my mom's high-heeled leather boots which came to my knees, black hot pants, and a tight sweater. I looked at myself in the mirror with astonishment. I looked vaguely like a Bond babe! The next day my blonde friends and I (always the dark-haired one) gathered together in the locker room to change into our costumes. One girl was in overalls, another wore a cute summer shorts outfit, and another had on a denim jacket and jeans. And then there was me. I was still nervous as I waited in the hall for my cue, but when I walked into the gym and heard the boys go wild, everything changed. Being a tough woman with sexual power was definitely the way to go! I began to move my image more and more in that direction, but with each step I lost more than I gained.

Let's go back and look a little more realistically at the Bond babes, the ones that ran with James. If I remember correctly, at least one of these women got knocked off, as in killed, in each 007 movie. In the end, James always bedded the remaining live one, but they were never seen together again. He was part of the next adventure, but they were not. There was always another beauty to pursue; once he slept with a woman, he was finished with her. I guess they truly were "bondwomen," daughters who forfeited their power when they gave in.

I know this rough, tough, and sexually confident woman might at first look brave to you, but she isn't. All bondwomen are afraid at one level or another, especially if they're not in control. (Why do you think they pack guns?) Many of them never got the protection and love they needed from their natural daddies when they were little girls, so they decided never to trust men again. Others were loved and nurtured, but they listened to a culture that encouraged them to trust in their beauty instead of in God, so they sought affirmation from numerous men. But eventually all bondwomen will find themselves on the outside looking in. Just because they are sexually desirable doesn't mean they were ever free.

> *⌒ All bondwomen are afraid at one level or another . . . (Why do you think they pack guns?)*

Nevertheless what does the Scripture say? "Cast out the bondwoman and her son, for the son of the bondwoman shall not be heir with the son of the freewoman." So then, brethren, we are not children of the bondwoman but of the free. (Gal. 4:30–31 NKJV)

Our culture gives us more opportunities to relate to the selfish, captive daughter than to the free woman. Like so many young girls, I spent one long Saturday afternoon at the matinee and watched the saga of *Gone with the Wind*. I know you won't be surprised if I tell you I wanted to be Scarlett . . . which is shocking since in the end she lost everything! I never dreamed of being the wimpy Melanie. If these were my only two choices, I certainly didn't want to be caught whining and fainting. But of course, they only wanted us to believe we had no other choices; you were either a nice, weak, fainting, compliant, flowery female who died young, or you were a strong, angry woman who killed as she chased after what she wanted, only to discover too late that she'd lost what she truly loved.

There *are* other options, and it is high time we learn what they are. There is a higher and more powerful way for women to adorn themselves. It requires no costumes (like me in my boot skit) or weapons of self-defense. This woman is much braver than any illusion portrayed by the sexual aggressor. Men do not

> ⟲ *There are other options, and it is high time we learn what they are.*

want to attack her; they long to be worthy of her. This one is a giver of life, not a taker. She is clothed in wisdom, and her apparel is always appropriate. She doesn't invite men to be base and aggressive but encourages them to be tender, careful, and wise.

I am afraid they do not regularly put this image of feminine mystique on the cover of women's magazines, so real-life, universally known examples are hard to come by. She is noble and rare, nothing like the flashy, common image in the grocery store. If I could choose a fitting wardrobe for her, I would have to go back in time to a lovelier setting. The beauty of her gown would flatter any wearer no matter her age or form. I could easily choose a gown from a Jane Austen movie, or the modern Cinderella story, *Ever After*, or even a costume from *Ben Hur* would do. It would be the furthest thing imaginable from a unisex garment, and it would embody the essence of femininity. The closest I've come to wearing something like this would be my wedding gown.

Many times while watching movies set in other eras, I've sighed and asked, *Why can't they make dresses like that today?* I am certain you know the type, and perhaps you have a favorite. They are so beautiful; there is almost a fear of touching and soiling them. Nothing about these outfits screams anything . . . but from head to toe they sing softly—lovely! Alluring yet modest. When I read the description of the garments of the saints in heaven, I discover that they are radiant with light and glory and luminous in texture. There is nothing earthbound or gaudy about them; they are altogether lovely.

Let's return to God's Word for His counsel in the area of purity of appearance. Because we are His, we should dress to please Him, regardless of whether we are single, widowed, divorced, or married. God has called us to be beautiful and fearless daughters of promise. To remain free, we choose to live by the Spirit, for it is the motive behind the directives in God's Word. Let's gather some New Testament Scriptures that address the issue of clothing. The first is found in Paul's instruction to Timothy:

> I also want women to dress modestly, with decency and propriety, not with braided hair or gold or pearls or expensive clothes, but with good deeds, appropriate for women who profess to worship God. (1 Tim. 2:9–10)

In my opinion, there are some big ideas here. First and foremost, a woman's dress is to be *modest;* this means void of pride and without the intent of drawing attention to itself. Second, it is to be *decent,* which means pure, moral, and virtuous. We are already well versed in its opposite . . . *indecent.* I have to be honest with you—sometimes I question the clothing I see on young girls and single women at church. I remember looking out of step when I first got saved because I only had a "heathen" wardrobe, but this is not what I am talking about. There is an alarming lack of modesty in daughters who have been raised in the church. I often have mothers of young boys plead with me, "Tell the young girls that how they dress is really affecting the young men!" The third description of dress in this passage is the word *propriety.* This is best defined as being appropriate and respectful of its setting. Just as a guest wearing gym clothes at a wedding would dishonor the bride and groom, we need to be sensitive to honor others with our choices of clothing.

Paul goes from there to the contrast between outer accessories and the adornment of good deeds. He is so otherworldly-minded because he has

> ⌒ *We need to be sensitive to honoring others with our choices of clothing.*

been to heaven, and knows what we have here doesn't compare with there. He is advising the woman, don't spend your time and resources on earthly treasures. Lay up for yourself treasures in heaven by adorning yourself with charitable acts.

We find another group of instructions for a Christian woman's wardrobe in 1 Peter:

> Do not let your adornment be merely outward—arranging the hair, wearing gold, or putting on fine apparel—rather let it be the hidden person of the heart, with the incorruptible beauty of a gentle and quiet spirit, which is very precious in the sight of God. For in this manner, in former times, the holy women who trusted in God also adorned themselves. (1 Peter 3:3–5 NKJV)

Peter says to not let your adornment be merely external, especially to the neglect of your internal beauty. Then he lets us into the beauty secret of the holy woman, that is, to cultivate a gentle and quiet spirit. A major factor in this adornment is learning to trust God. Paul encourages women to adorn themselves with good works, and Peter instructs them to focus on unseen treasure. If we develop our spirits like the holy women of old, we will put on the garment of grace and praise. These never wear out but grow more radiant with the passage of time.

> Abstain from all appearance of evil. (1 Thess. 5:22 KJV)

Our clothing should not even *appear to be* suggestive. This would eliminate much of any Bond girl's wardrobe. I'm sure I don't have to spell it out for you, but I will for the sake of clarity. Showing cleavage, navels, or excessive leg is not appropriate for church services, youth groups, or retreats. Neither are overly tight tops, pants, or dresses that leave nothing to the imagination. There really are not very many appropriate settings for such clothing. The clothing is not modest, because its whole intention is to call attention to breasts, navels, legs, or bottoms. It is not polite, because it can make others uncomfortable . . . especially hormone-driven, sight-oriented males. And it is not appropriate for those who profess to belong to God. I'm going to challenge you to take another look at your wardrobe and ask the Holy Spirit to be your fashion consultant. It will help if you ask yourself as you dress: *Is this modest? Is it decent? Is it appropriate for where I'm going? Does it honor whose I am? How am I affecting the males around me with my clothing? Am I honoring them and encouraging them in their pursuit of purity?*

> ⌒ *Your enemy wants to strip you, make sport of you, and merchandise your body.*

Your enemy wants to strip you, make sport of you, and merchandise your body, but your heavenly Father wants to clothe you with beauty, strength, dignity, and honor that will endure.

⌒ *Dear Heavenly Father,*

Clothe me in Your Son. I want to walk in the garments of dignity, strength, and honor. Give me wisdom and insight to walk not according to the pull of this world, but in accord with the purposes of heaven. Cover every area I have exposed in the shame of nakedness. I want to be a free daughter of promise. I renounce the influence and hold of the images of sexual aggression and seduction. Restore the innocence and beauty of my feminine mystique. I don't want to be naked and ashamed, but I want to be the one out dancing freely in the light.

Love,

Your Daughter

14 *Living Free from Regret*

To live a life free from regret, you must live your life on purpose, with an eye to the future. You cannot walk through this life without a dream or a destination in mind and expect to arrive just where you wanted to go. Too often we wake up to find ourselves where we did not wish to go, by a mode of transportation we did not enjoy. We may be tangled in the sheets of an uncomfortable bed, wondering how we ended up in this gloomy land of regret. Regret is a terrible destination, and the journey to it takes away so much of our life and strength. Because of this, the Bible offers lots of advice to avoid this nightmare, wisdom we will discuss later in this chapter.

Regret is an emotion with an incredible capacity for causing untold pain. It will shroud your heart with a leaden garment of despair and cause you to sink into the depths of hopelessness. As children, we are not as familiar with regret as we are with consequences. Childhood is a simpler time in our lives, when there is clear cause and effect . . . *if I do this, I will lose that.* Choices are laid out with careful thought to detail in order to assist children in making sound, intelligent decisions. When everything is clearly laid out, you will only make a bad choice if you think you can get away with it. But too often, we think just that.

> *You cannot walk through life without a dream or destination and expect to arrive just where you wanted to go.*

I remember as a five-year-old, I was forbidden to cross the street unless I was accompanied by my mother or by another older child. This was a source of untold embarrassment for me, even though my mother had clearly explained why it was so important that I followed her instructions. I understood we lived on a busy street and cars were capable of flattening me like a pancake . . . *but* the other kids only had to look both ways, while I required a private escort.

One day, I desperately wanted to go play at Jennifer's house across the street, so my mother walked me over, holding my hand all the way to the doorstep. I knocked on the door and heard giggles coming from within. I was certain they were laughing at my bodyguard. I waved good-bye to my mom and went in for a few hours of carefree bliss. When it was time to go home, Jennifer's mother offered her oldest daughter as an escort, but I had had enough! I let her know I was more than big enough to walk across the street by myself. Lying, I told her my mother had given me permission to walk home by myself. I threw my shoulders back and marched straight down their driveway, but even as I did, I had a horrible, sinking feeling in my stomach. I ignored it, looked both ways and crossed the street successfully. I had been careful not to cross within a clear view of my home, and once I was on my side of the street, I slinked along the tree line and ran hastily up to my door. I walked in just in time to see my mother hanging up the phone.

"Hi, Mom, I'm home!" I announced as I made a beeline for my bedroom.

"Just a minute," my mother stopped me in my tracks. "Sit down. I need to ask you something. Who walked you home today?"

The sinking feeling intensified. I glanced casually behind me to make sure she couldn't see the corner I had crossed at from our window before answering, "Cindy walked me home."

"Are you sure Cindy walked you home?" Mother probed further.

I nodded, not wanting to again speak a lie out loud.

"Should I call Mrs. Hoffman and ask her?"

I shook my head violently, "No!"

My mother then informed me Mrs. Hoffman had told her I had walked alone across the street. I was caught. I had not only disobeyed, I had lied. I was sent to sit in my room until my father came home.

Whenever I was sent to my room, I was not allowed to lie on the bed or play with my toys. I had to sit on a wooden stool that became more uncomfortable the longer I sat on it. I dreaded the return of my father. Each car that drove by brought with it another wave of terror . . . he was coming soon, and I was going to get it. During my time of solitude, I imagined all the different scenarios. Perhaps there wouldn't be a spanking . . . maybe my father would agree that I was big enough to cross the street by myself. The wait seemed to last forever.

Then he arrived. Normally when his car pulled in, I was there to meet him, so my absence could only mean two things: either I wasn't home, or I was in trouble. I heard my mother and father speaking in low voices to each other. I knew they were speaking of my crime. My stomach turned and I began to feel as though I would be ill. Then I heard footsteps in the hall. The door opened and there was my father's serious face.

"You can come out, Lisa. We need to talk to you."

I wiped away my tears and followed him down the hall like a lamb bound for the slaughter. Court was held in the living room. I sat by myself on the green chair, and my parents sat together across the room on the white sofa. They gave a lecture that I was incapable of hearing because their voices were drowned out by a more important question running through my mind, *Was I going to be spanked or not?*

I snapped back to reality when my father finally directly questioned me, "Did you disobey and lie about crossing the street?"

"Yes, yes!" I wept with heartfelt contrition, hoping somehow to sway the judge to be merciful. But the sentence had already been decided.

"You know what I have to do then, don't you?" my father would ask.

"Yes," I numbly answered. I knew I was getting it.

"Come on, let's get it over with." He motioned me over to him.

This meant I had to walk the suddenly vast expanse of the living room. I paused for a moment in the middle of the room to contemplate running out the front door, knowing that once I took the next step, I would pass the point of no return. I crept closer, stood before my father, and then bent over his knee. I got the swats, and when it was over . . . it was over.

My father held me in his lap as my mother told me how much she had always trusted me. How she wanted to trust me again and would. All the fear left my stomach, and I felt cleansed, loved, and accepted. Never again would I hear about my transgression. The next time I crossed the street I felt neither fear nor shame. I learned from my mistake and was disciplined for my transgression. I often wish it were so simple now.

> ∽ I learned from my mistake and was disciplined for my transgression. I often wish it were so simple now.

Far too often, regret goes deeper and endures longer than mere consequences of cause and effect. Regret continues to echo in our lives until it is finally addressed head-on. For the young child, regret is fleeting: *I shouldn't have done or said that,* and it often shows up immediately after the fact. But in adulthood, regret can behave differently, for we no longer have parents performing regular search-and-rescue operations for us. Too often in our youth, we become experts in covert operations, and we skillfully hide what we do. We reason, *What they don't know won't hurt them.* We foolishly believe no one will ever know about our secrets. But we do not realize a seed of regret has been planted, and it will continue to grow unnoticed in the soil of our youth. It waits until the plant is fully grown before making its way out of the shadows of our past and openly introducing itself at the most inopportune time.

Those of us who have known regret are well acquainted with its painful grip. It grabs our hands and does not let go until it has announced our folly to all those present. "Remember when . . . ?" Then it brings to the light for all to see something we had pushed far back into the shadows or something time itself had buried under the blanket of many years, perhaps even hiding it from our own memories. But now here it is for all to see, as though it had happened yesterday. And we hear our hearts moan, "If only!"

Regret is also capable of following quickly behind our mistakes. Something said or done yesterday in secret is suddenly and unexpectedly found exposed in the light today. A thoughtless word, a careless deed, a passing comment always weighs much heavier when it is rehearsed, gaining strength with each repetition. In the light of today, it always sounds harsher and looks glaringly different than it did in the soft focus of yesterday's intentions. We find ourselves wanting to defend it somehow: *I didn't mean it that way. You don't understand. It was different then.* We will always experience regret when we live for the moment and do not weigh our words and deeds before we give them life.

I have known regret, and I do not wish its sting in your life. I have known pain in the present because I walked in folly's counsel yesterday. I did not believe the things I now share with you. I had little or no understanding of consequences in my youth, and I believed the things I did under the cover of darkness would have little effect on me later. As your friend, I do not want to see you walk the same paths I've walked.

I believe each generation has the opportunity and mandate to redeem their mistakes by speaking the truth and warning the next generation. Daughters who become mothers have an opportunity to pass on a legacy of learning, so that, in turn, their daughters may stand higher, see clearer, and avoid the very pitfalls the mothers might have not avoided. This means we must bring the secrets from our pasts into our present so others may hear them and learn.

> ∽ *We will always experience regret when we live for the moment and do not weigh our words and deeds before we give them life.*

This is an invitation for you women who have known sexual regret to shine the light of truth on the dark paths so others will not have to walk them. It is a warning to others who are considering the path of promiscuity: *Steer clear. The price is too high, and the interest compounds with time.* To those who have chosen the path of light, blessing, and obedience, may this serve to guard you and strengthen your resolve. One way or another, if you live long enough, you find out one thing is certain: There is truly no such thing as a secret.

For there is nothing hidden that will not be disclosed, and nothing concealed that will not be known or brought out into the open. (Luke 8:17)

Notice, if you will, the word *nothing*. There is not a whole lot of margin for error with this word; *nothing* means *no thing*. Far too often, we read Scriptures like these and imagine

> ⌐ *When we say or do foolish or sinful things in secret, it is not God who embarrasses us; we embarrass ourselves.*

we are more clever or somehow excused from them, thus we refuse to grasp their meanings. We skip over them in our Bible reading and reason that God would never embarrass us.

But when we say or do foolish or sinful things in secret, it is not God who embarrasses us; we embarrass ourselves. It is like planting seeds in secret and then becoming angry with God when a plant appears. Perhaps on some level, we actually believe we are capable of hiding things well enough this verse doesn't really apply to our circumstances. But, if the Scripture says *no thing* will escape, it means without exception, everything hidden or concealed will be dug up and brought into the open light.

Given this insight, it is important we live with a greater awareness of our behavior. The book of Ephesians calls it living "circumspectly:"

> But all things that are exposed are made manifest by the light, for whatever makes manifest is light . . . See then that you *walk circumspectly*, not as fools but as wise. (Eph. 5:13–15 NKJV, emphasis added)

To live circumspectly means to live with the realization that the whole of our lives is connected, and more likely than not, the time will come when an event from our pasts will catch up to us in our future. The root of the word *circum* means "to go around" or "to encircle." To "spec" means "to see or to look at something" much like a builder "specs" a home so potential customers may examine his quality and skill before they purchase it. Likewise, we are charged to live our lives, weighing out our decisions and actions from every angle and point of view. We need to take a walk around our decisions, visit every room, and be certain we like the way it looks and feels from every angle before we commit ourselves to it long term. But I am not certain most of us really believe this to be necessary.

When I moved to Colorado, I went shopping for a sofa for my family room. I remember finding one I really liked. I thought, *Here is the perfect sofa*. It looked great backed up against the wall of the furniture store, surrounded by beautiful accessories and paintings. But then I remembered my sofa would not have a wall behind it. It would need to look good standing on its own, from the back as well as from the front. When I pulled the sofa away from the wall, I realized it wasn't going to work after all. Had I only looked at the front of the sofa, I would have taken it home, sat in it, and congratulated myself on its comfort and beauty. I would have loved it . . . until I walked into my kitchen and caught a glimpse of its backside.

Most of us only see the inviting portions of a thing. We like the way it looks, the way it feels, and say to ourselves, *after all, I deserve all the pleasure and satisfaction it affords . . . I'll take it!* Only later do we check our backsides and experience the embarrassment.

> ◡ *Never in my wild phase did I imagine the pain I'd experience twenty years later.*

When I was an unrestrained youth, I reasoned myself into believing I should freely give myself whatever I desired. After all, I was a college girl, full grown and capable of voting, driving, and choosing a lifelong profession . . . life was an adventure calling out loudly to me. Never once in my wild phase did I imagine the pain I'd experience some twenty years later as I looked upon the earnest faces of my two oldest sons when they asked the probing question, "Mom, you were a virgin when you married Dad . . . right?" Their sweet voices did not accuse me, but they were seeking an affirmation of the virtue they never doubted their mother possessed — the very one I would have to honestly deny.

In the heat of those passionate moments in college, I never even dreamed such questions would exist for me. If I had been insightful enough back then to consider the future, I would likely not have taken foolish pride in my sexual conquests. Yet pride was quite possibly the farthest emotion from what I was experiencing at that moment. I felt immediately torn between several choices. I could lie and tell them I had been a virgin on my wedding day, or I could tell them it was none of their business, thus skirting the issue and avoiding being honest. I also had the option of making the classic Christian excuse for my behavior: I wasn't a Christian when I lost my virginity. I didn't know better! Or I could choose the most painful option, the ugly naked truth. I took a deep breath and answered truthfully, "No, I was not, and I regret it to this day. I believe your inheritance will be very different from mine."

Anything less than honest answers will undermine the power and ability of our children to walk in purity. Truth breeds freedom as surely as shame propagates lies. You don't have to give details of your exploits, for it is possible to tell the truth without providing full disclosure.

At this point, you may raise the argument: *I am forgiven and have become a new creation. The old has passed away, and all things have become new for me.* Of course, this is the ultimate truth of the Word of God. I do believe I am forgiven. I do believe my sins were washed away when I confessed them. I do believe I was made new and have experienced the overwhelming mercy of Christ. But this does not mean all by-products from my previous choices have been eliminated. I am no longer guilty and under judgment, but some consequences remain. If my children break a vase, I forgive them, but the vase remains broken.

> ∼ *Anything less than honest answers will undermine the power and ability of our children to walk in purity.*

For the sake of further argument, let's consider a hypothetical situation. What if I had become pregnant during my wild single days? Perhaps this would have served as a wake-up call to me. I became a Christian while pregnant. Even though I had experienced the love and mercy of Christ, would the baby in my womb disappear? No, of course not! But the existence of the child would not negate the forgiveness of my sin, just as the forgiveness of my sin would not erase the existence of the child. There would remain fruit from the seeds I'd planted and by-products of the choices I had made. But I would have loved and celebrated the life of this child, even if his or her conception had taken place outside of marriage.

Here is a real-life case. When I was first married, I traveled as a promotional representative for a cosmetic firm. There were three reps in Dallas and three in Houston. A few of us were Christians, and we loved it when we had the opportunity to travel together and fellowship over lunch and dinner.

One of the more beautiful single Christian representatives was having a lot of health problems and terrible anxiety attacks. I feared she would lose her job because she continually called in sick and lagged behind in her duties and energy on the job.

One night we were together at a promotion, and I asked her if we could pray together. I was afraid she was heading down a path of despair and destruction, and I really hoped somehow through prayer her arrival at this destination could be averted. She had everything going for her, a church home, a company car, good pay, great benefits, fun travel, but she was never happy. I asked her, "Why?" and she opened up to me.

"You don't understand. You're married, I'm not. You don't know what it is like to always be lonely."

I encouraged her to get involved in her church, stop complaining, and start being thankful for what she did have.

"It doesn't work for me. I've tried it, and I travel too much. I'm so tired when I get home I spend my entire weekend recovering from my week" she said.

After a while, it seemed no matter what I said, she maneuvered around it one way or another. It was getting late, and we hadn't even prayed, but I had become discouraged and was imagining her situation impossible as well.

"Let's pray . . . you go first," I suggested.

We joined hands, and she began to pray. But as she prayed, I wasn't even hearing what she said. I was seeing something very different. The Holy Spirit was showing me something so clearly it was almost frightening to me. If I told her what I seeing, but I was wrong, I would be totally out of line.

I promised God I would speak if given the opportunity. The image faded, and I was listening again to my friend pray. She was crying out to God, "Please, please, God forgive me!"

"He has," I answered.

"No," she countered. "He doesn't forgive me. I ask, and He doesn't do it."

I squeezed her hand, opened my eyes, and looked into hers.

"I know why you *think* God doesn't forgive you."

"No, you don't understand. I *know* He hasn't forgiven me!"

I took a deep breath and continued, "You think God hasn't forgiven you because He hasn't healed you of genital herpes."

She was shocked and whispered back, "How did you know?"

"I didn't. God just showed me. He wanted you to know how much He loves you. Just because you haven't been healed, it doesn't mean you haven't been forgiven."

Then she shared her sad, tragic story with me, and everything finally made sense. She had been raised as a Christian all her life, but one night she found herself at a party she knew she shouldn't be at. She was uncomfortable and started drinking to feel a little more relaxed in the unfamiliar atmosphere. Sensing she was uncomfortable, an attractive man moved in, befriended her, gave her a lot of attention, and told her how beautiful she was. Before she knew what had happened, she found herself alone with him. Things began to heat up, but she thought she could keep things under control. She didn't realize how hard it can be to keep things under control when two people are partially undressed, slightly intoxicated, and by themselves. She said no, but he wasn't listening, and no one else was there to stop him. That evening she lost her virginity and gained the incurable venereal disease, genital herpes. Years had passed since then, but she was still plagued with guilt and shame.

> ⌒ *She had lived so long under the weight of regret, she'd turned around and blamed it on God.*

"The very first time I ever did anything I got it! My friends were messing around all the time, and all of them are fine. Most of them are even married now," she wept.

"God didn't show me this to condemn you, but to let you know He has heard your cries, knows your pain, and forgives you. Why else would He show me this but to reach out to you?" I reaffirmed.

That night, she let go of her anger with God and received His forgiveness. She had lived so long under the weight of regret, she'd turned around and blamed it on God. Before that, every time she had relapsed, she feared it was God condemning her for her sins, and she felt the violation anew. That night, we prayed for the release of guilt from her, as well as for her healing—spirit, soul, and body.

That was many years ago. I have not spoken with her in nearly twenty years. I do not know if she is healed physically or not, but I do know a healing of her heart began that night. Do I believe God can heal her physically as well? Yes, nothing is impossible for God, but when the heart is broken, it becomes His first concern.

Now, let's look at another lonely figure. She sits at the end of a weathered pier. The wind whips her dark hair about her face as she struggles to push it behind her ears and retrieve it from her tear-filled eyes. Her legs are pulled up to her chest to keep the wind from the book in her lap. Yet the pages blow wildly in the wind, and she frantically wrestles them in search of some comfort or answers, but finds none.

She straightens up from her ball of shame and tilts her face upward, no longer pushing aside the wayward hair, she allows it to whip her face in punishment. At twenty-two, she is overwhelmed with the reality of her choices. She believes God is merciful, but at the same time, she fears her sins are too great. Tonight she will have to answer for the very things she imagined buried in the depths of the sea.

Noticing the lateness of the hour, she prays one last desperate prayer, and leaves. As she walks back to her car, she vows to be brave and honest. Tonight she must face the man she loves; she is certain he is about to ask her to marry him, but before he does, he must know the truth about her. She imagines again his disappointment . . . for this young man is a virgin, one who saved himself for his wife. He deserves better than the likes of her, and tonight she will tell him so.

Returning to her dismal, empty, one-room efficiency apartment, she showers and prepares for their time together. She'd told him the night before she needed to speak with him and asked if they could go for a walk instead of going out somewhere. She wanted to be away from the eyes and ears of strangers when she told him.

His apartment is a few blocks away, and she wants to spend some time walking alone before they walk together. She rehearses her sad truth aloud to the wind and shudders as the words pass her lips. Sooner than she is ready, she is at his door.

She knocks a little hesitantly, wondering if this will be the last time she'll be welcomed inside. A voice inside bids her to come in, and before her is the best friend she's ever known. He immediately senses her struggle and rises to enfold her in his arms, but she puts her hand out to maintain a measured distance between them. She fears if he holds her, she will not be brave enough to tell him the truth.

She looks around nervously, "Where is your roommate?"

"He's out with the guys . . . are you all right?"

"No, I'm not. I'll feel better after we talk."

"Okay, let me get my shoes, and we'll go . . . but do you mind if I read you a Scripture? I felt impressed to share it with you."

She nods numbly and actually trembles as he turns away to leaf through his Bible. What could God possibly say to her? She'd cried out to Him all day long for a single whisper and heard nothing over the noise of her own conscience. After all, if it condemned her, didn't God as well?

"Here it is. It's kind of off the wall. I hope it doesn't offend you."

"Go ahead," She answers.

"Well, I know you already know this, but here it goes: 'Therefore, if anyone is in Christ, he is a new creation; old things have passed away; behold, all things have become new'" (2 Cor. 5:17 NKJV). He continued, "I know this sounds weird, but I felt like God said to tell you old things had been made new, and you were like . . . a virgin."

She stutters back a response, and her eyes filled with tears, "Well, I'm *not* a virgin. That's what I was going to tell you."

He stands before her now, a hand on each shaking shoulder, "If God says you are . . . who are we to argue?"

She shakes her head in disbelief and relief and begins to weep. He pulls her to his chest and lets her cry until the storm is past and she feels cleansed.

"Let's go for that walk."

"Thanks," she answers.

The two walk for hours that night, and together they watch the sun set on the shameful secret that had threatened to separate them. God's mercy truly endures forever. That was almost twenty years ago, and John and I have been together ever since.

Now you know why I wish with all my heart that you would never have to wrestle with the ghosts of your past the way I did. Some of you may already be in my shoes. It is time to face the storm and turn aside to the truth. It is time to turn from your sin in repentance, let it break your heart, and give the Prince the pieces. He is merciful and has tender compassion for women who have been rejected and outcast.

> ⌒ *It is time to turn from your sin in repentance, let it break your heart, and give the Prince the pieces.*

I want to share a portion of a beautiful letter written from one mother to her daughter, because I want you to glimpse the beauty of sexual purity without regret.

> *It is my desire these truths will motivate you to remain pure as a woman of God . . . I have come to realize one reason I so enjoy being intimate with your father is because I knew no shame. This is because I was given guidance and knew the value of purity when I was young. I knew it was a treasure. God gave me a man who'd remained pure and honored my purity during our engagement. When I enjoy intimacy with your father, the wedding dress on our bedroom wall is a symbol of our purity that remains even today. I find myself praising God for this gift I enjoy so freely.*

There is no regret in her words—only joy. I want that for you. If you have sinned, the only way to remove this shadow from your life is to let it pierce any hardness of heart with godly sorrow, then allow the power of repentance to lead you to salvation.

> Godly sorrow brings repentance that leads to salvation and leaves no regret, but worldly sorrow brings death. (2 Cor. 7:10)

What exactly is worldly sorrow? It is to grieve about the loss of worldly things, including one's reputation, money, possessions, relationships, or other worldly things. It focuses on one's own losses without realizing the pain caused to others or to God. It attempts to bring about change in its own strength through religious efforts, without ever going to the root of the motives of the heart. The best scriptural example of worldly sorrow would be Judas.

> *Godly sorrow moves beyond consequences and focuses on our relationships with God.*

Godly sorrow moves beyond the concern of consequences and focuses on our relationships with God. It is a rending of a veil so we can see things as they really are. David gives us the best example of this with his words in Psalm 51:1:

> Have mercy on me, O God, according to your unfailing love; according to your great compassion blot out my transgressions.

David lifts his eyes to God and appeals to His unfailing love for the removal of his transgressions. Then, he confesses his sin as sin against God.

> Against you, you only, have I sinned and done what is evil in your sight, so that you are proved right when you speak and justified when you judge. (Ps. 51:4)

There is no defense of his actions or blaming of others here. He openly acknowledges his sin. When we openly own up to things, we are openly cleansed. When we need the depths of mercy (and who among us honestly doesn't?), we are to humble ourselves so God may exalt us out of our circumstances.

Cleanse me with hyssop, and I will be clean; wash me, and I will be whiter than snow. (Ps. 51:7)

David is moving away from his son now as he asks for cleansing. He acknowledges he cannot clean himself, but again he turns to the Lord for the removal of not only his sin but also every trace or shadow of its stain.

Create in me a pure heart, O God, and renew a steadfast spirit within me. (Ps. 51:10)

His sin is cleansed, and he begins to ask for the empowering grace of a pure heart and a steadfast spirit to be quickened again within him. David understood sin has a way of dulling the heart and weakening the resolve of our spirits to serve God. Then he progresses, asking:

Restore to me the joy of your salvation and grant me a willing spirit, to sustain me. Then I will teach transgressors your ways, and sinners will turn back to you. (Ps. 51:12–13)

These last three verses are quite possibly my favorites in this psalm. They contain a promise of restored joy where there has been regret and sorrow. They give a promise of a new beginning to make something beautiful out of something ugly. They provide the opportunity to teach other transgressing pilgrims of the faithful mercy and love of God and to see them restored as well. May our heavenly Father transform every dark place of regret into shining beacons of His faithfulness and truth. May

> *May our heavenly Father transform every dark place of regret into shining beacons of His faithfulness and truth.*

He triumph in your redemption. May you in turn change every place of pain into examples of beauty and freedom by teaching transgressors about the Word that has been made flesh in your life.

Let's review Psalm 51:

1. We appeal to God based on His mercy, not on our merit.

2. We confess the issue as a sin against Him.

3. We acknowledge His judgments as righteous.

4. We ask for His cleansing and accept it as a done deal.

5. We ask Him to purify any defilement and renew our spirits.

6. We ask for the joy of His salvation.

7. We commit to teach others from our mistakes and walk in humility.

I no longer wish I had made different decisions, even though I wish a different experience for every daughter of God who holds this book. I am overwhelmed by the mercy of our Father, who has allowed my sins to be your warning, my restoration to be your hope, my freedom to be your release. Pray with David:

⌒ *Dear Heavenly Father,*

Have mercy on me, O God, according to your unfailing love; according to your great compassion blot out my transgressions. Wash away all my iniquity and cleanse me from my sin. For I know my transgressions, and my sin is always before me. Against you, you only, have I sinned and done what is evil in your sight, so that you are proved right when you speak and justified when you judge . . . you desire truth in the inner parts; you teach me wisdom in the inmost place. Cleanse me with hyssop, and I will be clean; wash me, and I will be whiter than snow. Let me hear joy and gladness; Create in me a pure heart, O God, and renew a steadfast spirit within me. Do not cast me from your presence or take your Holy Spirit from me. Restore to me the joy of your salvation and grant me a willing spirit, to sustain me. Then I will teach transgressors your ways, and sinners will turn back to you . . . my tongue will sing of your righteousness. O Lord, open my lips, and my mouth will declare your praise. The sacrifices of God are a broken spirit; a broken and contrite heart, O God, you will not despise. (Ps. 51:1–17)

15 Why We Lose When We Give In

The unfair, ugly fact about the mating dance is that so much of female sexual power depends upon withholding oneself. If anything, that is even truer in an age when all the other girls are available, too.[1]
—LISA SCHIFFREN, *THE WOMEN'S QUARTERLY*

*H*ow thought provoking to find this sentiment in the writings of a secular journal. It appears all things old are becoming new, and God is much more of an advocate for women than we've been led to believe. Even the secular world is waking up to the angry voice of a disillusioned generation of women who are admitting promiscuity didn't really get them what they wanted. As women, we lose so much more than the men when we give in.

> *⌐ This is about the restoration of dignity, honor, strength, and yes . . . even power to a generation of women, young and old, who are no longer willing to lose.*

Of course, these sages suggest moderating our approach merely for the sake of gaining our dearest desires. But this will not be enough. For us there is a higher calling. This isn't about modifying our behavior in order to get what we want. This is about the restoration of dignity, honor, strength, and yes . . . even power to a generation of women, young and old, who are no longer willing to lose.

Listen to this telling insight from Danielle Crittenden's eye-opening book, *What Our Mothers Didn't Tell Us*:

Indeed, in all the promises made to us about our ability to achieve freedom and independence as women, the promise of sexual emancipation may have been the most illusory. These days, certainly, it is the one most brutally learned. All the sexual bravado a girl may possess evaporates the first time a boy she truly cares for makes it clear that he has no further use for her after his own body has been satisfied. No amount of feminist posturing, no amount of reassurances that she doesn't need a guy like that anyway, can protect her from the pain and humiliation of those awful moments after he's gone, when she's alone and feeling not sexually empowered but discarded.[2]

The horror of being used then tossed aside is especially disconcerting when mere youths are experiencing this extreme magnitude of rejection. We were never meant to be thrown away, but embraced especially after completely giving, unveiling, and revealing ourselves. We were never meant to be left after allowing an entrance to our most intimate place. Sexual union was meant to be the culmination, celebration, and cementing of two becoming one. It was never meant to be the last act before parting. How terrible to hear, "I got what I wanted; now I'm out of here . . . Oh, by the way, thanks."

Our wombs were meant for carefully and lovingly planted seeds of life, not for careless ones cast in darkness. Our wombs are like gardens and meant to be tended so they can flourish. God charged the newlywed men of Israel to stay home the entire first year of marriage just to bring happiness to their new wives (Deut. 24:5 NIV). She was to be securely planted in a garden of happiness where she could blossom and from which life would come forth.

As women, we were created to be so much more than an outlet of sexual release for men. As women, we want and deserve more than just sexual release for ourselves . . . we crave intimacy, romance, and passion. We want to know and be known. There can be no intimacy where there is no trust, and there can be no lasting trust where there is no covenant. How can you possibly trust someone who gives you no reason to believe that he will be there tomorrow? If he is not willing to wait for you today, to lay aside his immediate sexual passions, he will not wait around for

> *We crave intimacy, romance, and passion. We want to know and be known.*

you tomorrow. Men are conquerors by nature: When they have enjoyed the fullness of the spoils, they move on to the next challenge.

There is another quirky twist in male and female relationships. It is almost impossible to begin with sexual contact and then upgrade to a deeper realm of intimacy. Men are not interested in knowing more thoroughly those they have already known too quickly, no matter how many movies may suggest otherwise. Why take the time to examine closer the label of a wine bottle you've already emptied?

A man loves adventure, intrigue, and a woman who challenges him to be more because she believes there is more. He wants to believe in the one who believes in him. He wants to know he can trust her with his heart, his children, and his money. Deep down inside, good men desire to be someone's prince or knight in shining armor. If you are waiting for your prince, never forget that he will be looking for a princess.

Let's go back for now to what we as women stand to lose through promiscuity:

Losses: respect, virginity, power, exclusivity, mystery, innocence, trust, good reputation, control, sexual health, purity, fertility, trust, freedom, and future of the relationship.

From a biological standpoint, it is of course the woman who becomes pregnant, not the man. He can walk away from the child without the shedding of blood, but she cannot. It is the woman who either carries a fatherless child to term or kills it while it grows within her. It is the woman who must bear a child she might have to give away. It is a woman who, if she keeps the child, must one day explain to that little one why his or her father didn't care enough to stay. These are all painful choices.

Many STDs (Sexually Transmitted Diseases) ravage a woman's reproductive system before they are even detectable. This often means she will have a hard time getting pregnant if she is not already sterile. Then there is the issue of the AIDS virus, which cuts short our very lives. Men can often move from one sexual liaison to another much more quickly than women, and they can pass on more than just their seed before they even realize what has happened.

One busy young man happened to impregnate both a young girl I know and her best friend's sister in the same week. They had their babies just days apart. And where was this young man while these girls were writhing in the pain of childbirth? Was he holding their hands? No, he'd skipped town.

Now let's count a woman's potential gains from sexual promiscuity:

Gains: temporary pleasure and sexual experience

Let's look at the gains and losses for the man:

Losses: virginity and sexual health

Gains: temporary pleasure, sexual experience, thrill of conquest, freedom to move on to someone else

You can see this drama played out every afternoon on daytime television. I happened upon a talk show the other day, and the banner under the concerned face of a fifteen-year-old girl read something like "Thinks he is the father of her baby." It appeared there was a paternity question. The boy had agreed to blood work to prove his innocence, and live on the air they would either nail him or clear his name with the results. The envelope was opened as though it were the announcement of an Academy Award recipient. "And the results are . . . (drum roll please) . . . you are *not* the father!" The young man leaped out of his seat and began to jump up and down with joy! "I'm going home free! I'm free! All right I told you . . .you ———, that wasn't my baby!" After high-fiving some friends in the audience, he continued his celebration backstage while the large monitor behind the host and this young girl showed it all.

What struck me was the horror on this young girl's face. She looked utterly lost and hopeless. Even the host sensed her fear, and he leaned over, took her hand, and said, "Forget about him. We're going to help you." The girl nodded numbly while the image of a young man set free continued to jump and jeer behind her.

I have to admit it. I saw it and burst into tears. How can her life ever be the same? She had brought her case before the media of this nation with the hope of securing a father for her child, only to find out there was not one. Of course, this begs the question, Why didn't she bring in all the boys she'd slept with during that time period? Perhaps he was the only one she cared enough for to tie her life to. The truth she sought out had offered her no protection. She was shamed and left utterly powerless before millions of detached strangers. The immediate reaction of the studio audience was mixed. Some were stunned, some shook their heads, and others laughed her to scorn. I just wished I could have held her.

I can't do this for her, but I can warn you. The price of promiscuity for men is miniscule in comparison to the cost it exacts upon women. I believe this is part of the struggle brought upon us in the transgression of the garden.

> ~ *The price of promiscuity for men is miniscule in comparison to the cost it exacts from women.*

It is just another example of how women suffer when the laws of love are desecrated. These laws were never put in place to steal your joy and pleasure but to protect it. Sin definitely has pleasure for a season. I am certain that the young girl enjoyed momentary pleasure in the arms of this young man just as she had apparently found in the arms of others as well, but that fleeting ecstasy was nothing in comparison with what she must have felt that day on TV.

When you begin with what was meant to be the culmination of a union, then everything moves rapidly downhill from there. If the most intense level (the sexual) is developed first to the neglect of other areas of the relationship, it will lack the cement that would hold it together. A man does not have to search hard or far to find a woman who is available for sex. In today's society he will usually not even have to pay money for her services.

I want to share a cartoon I read long ago in college in a pornographic men's magazine. A man and woman are in bed, about to have sex. She places her hand up to stop his progress until he answers her question, "Will you still respect me in the morning?" In the next frame, he looks confused, "Respect you in the morning? I don't respect you now!"

If you are looking for respect, you will not find it in promiscuity. Men still prefer to marry women who haven't slept with anyone, especially not with someone they know. Men like to bed, flirt with, and sometimes even date a wild child, but those women aren't usually first on their lists for marriage or motherhood.

Promiscuity gives women the freedom to behave sexually like a man. But the truth is, regardless of how we behave, we will never be men . . . so why should we act like them? Women are at their strongest when they embrace their feminine mystique.

Of course, our culture has done its best to tie the term *feminine* to a sissy, weak, and wimpy image. I suppose that when you apply feminine aspects to men, they do look out of place. But femininity is not out of step for women. When women stand in the strength of their roles as women, men are challenged to rise to a new level or standard in their roles. Men crave the respect, affection, and attention of those whom they feel are their equal but complementary other halves. It is not good for men to be alone, for their labor and lives have no real purpose without someone to share it with. Men are not inspired to protect women who are naked, but instead to conquer and violate them; they want to protect those who are clothed.

If we want to regain intimacy then we must be reconciled to truth. If we want back our dignity and respect then we must be willing to put back on our clothing. All of the sexual liberation has not elevated but degraded the image of women. You can have seduction without the influence of femininity, but femininity carries with it the allure of feminine mystique.

For centuries, the daughters of Eve have cried out to the sons of Adam, *Give me sacrificial love. Rescue and protect me. Meet my deepest need for security and safety.* When the son of Adam

> *All of the sexual liberation has not elevated but degraded the image of women.*

answers, he makes declarations he cannot keep in the hope that she will meet a yearning he cannot verbalize. Both are doomed to fail because God alone wants to meet those deep desires in each of us.

In desperation we have prostituted ourselves, wrestled, and waged war with the sons of Adam in an attempt to get them to bless us and affirm our value. But this struggle has left us frustrated at best. Far too often we are left disappointed in the dust, raped, wounded, and alone. In the end, it is all a senseless and exhausting process in which both parties lose. It is not the fault of the sons of Adam; they cannot give us the blessing we seek, and we have frightened them by giving them so much power over our souls. We must learn the blessings we truly need come only from God. We must allow God to give us a new name, for we are no longer daughters of Eve, hiding in the shadows, but daughters of light and promise, His bride.

In John Eldredge's excellent book, *Wild at Heart* (Thomas Nelson Publishers, 2001), he shares the common disappointment men experience when they look for their fulfillment from what he calls "the fair-haired maiden." Ah, but what of us women? Is not our guilt even greater? For we have looked too long at Adam only to be let down. Adam was before Eve. And Adam is still before her. Adam represents a preeminence woman will never know, because he was first. Eve truly looked to Adam to be so much more than a husband. He was her brother and a type of father, for she was the only woman born of man. She was disappointed by Adam's choice, just as she was disappointed in her own. We really do want men who draw their strength from something bigger than us.

Adam can never break our chains. When you look only to Adam, you will struggle and be disappointed. But when you look to God, you are no longer a naked and shamed daughter of Eve, but you are a clothed and redeemed daughter of promise . . . a glorious bride who sings and dances while she waits for her prince. You can be passionate, because you have exchanged law for longing, bondage for freedom, and rules for relationship. You are a royal woman. Some women have known the bitterness of regret before experiencing the joyous flood of mercy. This is an urgent call for women to return to their original position of strength, dignity, and honor. With our heads held high, we can declare freedom to our sisters and daughters; yes we can release them to go and sin no more!

> ⌒ *Adam can never break our chains. When you look only to Adam, you will struggle and be disappointed.*

Conclusion *The Power of Love*

I am in my twentieth year of marriage, but if I reach back I can still remember what it felt like to be a bride. I am not talking about the tedious tasks and financial burden of planning a wedding—these were never meant to be on the shoulders of the bride—for brides were always meant to be swept away. No, I speak of the joy of love anticipated and openly celebrated by all. I remember counting down the days to when my life would depart from what I'd known, and I'd embark on the journey of my dreams. Would my life be as I'd imagined? Since all of us are His bride, it is important to understand how brides should think.

- A bride longs to run away with her bridegroom to a secret and beautiful place, far away from the eyes and noise of others. In this quiet privacy she longs to be loved with more than words.

- A bride aches for the touch of her bridegroom. He's awakened feelings and passion deep within her that only his touch may satisfy. She longs to be embraced and to respond with abandonment.

- A bride loves to have a special song she shares only with her bridegroom—a tune that embodies their love and becomes "their" song.

- A bride loves the sound of her bridegroom's voice—especially when he tenderly whispers to her. Then she knows it is reserved for her alone.

- A bride longs to be beautifully arrayed and when ready, tenderly undressed.

- A bride longs to stand before her bridegroom naked and unashamed. She wants to feel every part of her body is beautiful and desirable to Him . . . her shape and form is just what he'd hoped for.

- A bride longs to please her bridegroom in every way.

- A bride desires to be pure and passionate in all she does.

- A bride longs to speak and be truly heard, not in the simple words of this language, but in the complex tongue of the heart. She desires to be understood at a depth she cannot even communicate.

- A bride needs to feel safe when she makes herself vulnerable.

- A brides loves the freedom to express herself without fear.

- A bride delights in surprises and unexpected gifts.

- A bride loves to share secrets with her bridegroom.

- A bride loves to be chased by her beloved and then chase him in return.

- A bride loves knowing the joy of belonging.

- A bride desires to be nurtured, protected, directed, and even gently corrected, but never criticized. When she feels criticized, she ceases to flourish and shrinks from the touch of her beloved.

- A bride is not interested in other loves, for she is consumed with her first one.

If these descriptions break your heart . . . let them. It is God breaking up the fallow and hard ground and saying, "Let Me love you." These longings are found in every woman . . . they run so deep no earthly man can satisfy them all. Sons of Adam may sometimes satisfy some of these needs, but other longings will remain neglected. Though earthly love may escape or disappoint you, the truth is, you long for another. This heavenly Prince will never disappoint or hurt you. He forged your deepest desires and has always been your dream, just as you have been His.

As a bridegroom rejoices over his bride, so will your God rejoice over you. (Isa. 62:5)

Readying yourself for your bridegroom has never been a quiet, passive rite of passage; it has always meant a time of passion—a transition from the bride's world to the world of her beloved. You join an ancient procession that rejoices and trembles with excitement . . . the elite daughters of heaven who long to hear God's voice and revel in His embrace.

I have gone to great lengths to show you the care with which God searches out His bride. I want you to glimpse the depths and lengths God would go to in order to secure you for His Son. You can never truly be His until you know His unfailing love. He must capture our hearts so He might sweep us away. For where our treasure is, so our hearts reside as well.

I delight greatly in the LORD; my soul rejoices in my God. For he has clothed me with garments of salvation and arrayed me in a robe of righteousness, as a bridegroom adorns his head like a priest, and as a bride adorns herself with her jewels. (Isa. 61:10)

Cover your nakedness with His salvation. Wrap yourself in His righteousness. Adorn yourself with the jewels of His adoration. Revel in His embrace, and let your heart dance before Him.

⌒ *Dear Heavenly Father,*

Quicken me. I am Yours. Let me glimpse Your love and know Your touch. I want to behold You and be captivated by Your gaze. Set me like a seal on Your heart. Hold me close, and never let me go. I love you, my beautiful and glorious Prince. Beautify me with your salvation. Come quickly, Lord Jesus.

Love,

Your Daughter

Notes

CHAPTER 9

1. *Matthew Henry's Commentary on the Whole Bible: New Modern Edition, Electronic Database* (Hendrickson Publishers, Inc., 1991).
2. Ibid.

CHAPTER 14

1. Lisa Schriffen, *The Women's Quarterly* 1997, 97.
2. Danielle Crittenden, *What Our Mothers Didn't Tell Us* (New York: Touchstone, 1999), 31.

About the Author

*L*isa Bevere is the bestselling author of *Out of Control and Loving It; The True Measure of a Woman; Be Angry, But Don't Blow It!; and You Are Not What You Weigh*. A popular speaker and frequent radio and TV guest, Lisa lives in Colorado, where she carpools her four sons and enjoys time with her husband, John, a bestselling author as well.

Acknowledgments

Jesus, my ultimate Prince and Savior. You clothed my nakedness with dignity, my shame with honor. My limited words and actions could never adequately express the depth of my gratitude and affection. May Your precious Word always be flesh in my life so others may glimpse Your beauty.

To my husband, John. Twenty years ago you looked beyond my shame and saw beauty, then stole me from my nightmare and transported me to a dream . . . thank you.

To my four sons, Addison, Austin, Alec, and Arden, for all the times you've shared me with others through writing and speaking. May God multiply all you've sown and give each of you the dreams in your hearts, for each of you is truly a delight to mine.

Kristen Lucas, for your listening ear, words of encouragement, and skillful editing.

Victor Oliver, for your wisdom to provoke me deeper.

Belinda Bass, for letting me bounce ideas off of you.

Pamela Clements, for your laughter when things were heavy.

Mike Hyatt, for demanding a "Big Idea."

To all those unnamed who lent their gifts and talents to this project . . . may it set captives free.

Other Books by Lisa Bevere

Be Angry, But Don't Blow It!
Out of Control and Loving It!
The True Measure of a Woman
Pathway to His Presence
You Are Not What You Weigh

Books by John Bevere

A Heart Ablaze
The Bait of Satan
Breaking Intimidation
The Devil's Door
The Fear of the Lord
Thus Saith the Lord?
Under Cover
Victory in the Wilderness
The Voice of One Crying

Be Angry, But Don't Blow It!
Maintaining Your Passion Without Losing Your Cool

BY LISA BEVERE

Conflict—it's unavoidable. Therefore each of us must learn to manage it successfully. But what if we can't? What if anger has us out of control and out of hand? You're passionate and losing your cool. Or perhaps worse—you're depressed and wrought with fear because you've turned the destructive force of rage on yourself.

This book interweaves powerful scriptural truths with practical, personal examples and prayer. Readers will learn to channel passionate emotions constructively. Anger is not wrong; it is how we express it and how far we take it that determines the outcome. For those really ready to be honest and get free, this book will light the way. **ISBN: 0-7852-6988-6**

Under Cover:
The Key to Living in God's Provision and Protection

BY JOHN BEVERE

This well-loved writer effectively uses examples of his personal mistakes to illustrate riveting truths about repentance and forgiveness. As he focuses on the true authority of God, he is careful to explain by example the important difference between submission and obedience.

The same struggle with divine authority is also represented through the lives of John the Baptist, the apostle Paul, and other biblical figures. An especially helpful book for Christians who want to develop a serious pursuit of God. **ISBN: 0-7852-6991-6**

To receive JBM's free newsletter, *The Message,* and to receive a free color catalog of ministry resources, please contact:

John Bevere Ministries
P.O. Box 888
Palmer Lake, CO 80133-0888
1-800-648-1477
(U.S. Only)
E-mail: jbm@johnbevere.org
Web site: www.johnbevere.org

In Europe, please contact the ministry at:

John Bevere Ministries International Ltd.
P.O. Box 2794
WALSALL
WS2 7YQ
United Kingdom
Telephone: 44 (0) 870 745 5790
Facsimile: 44 (0) 870 745 5791
E-mail: jbmeurope@johnbevere.org

The Messenger television program airs on the Christian Channel Europe. Please check your local listings for day and time.